AWARENESS MANTRA

BY

Pranoy Mukherjee

TABLE OF CONTENTS

I dedicate this book to....

My Family

Naked Reality discord group

Luv Jaiswal

Vrajras Das

Quora followers

All those on the journey of self improvement

INTRODUCTION

I am glad you decided to read this book! This is not your regular self-help book. You won't find much of sugar-coated motivations in here. This book strives to expose 'you' to yourself. It cuts right to the heart of the matter and lays the truth bare for you to witness and apply. It's focussed on deep understanding and practical application alike.

Whether you are new to self-development or in the advanced stages, this book will help you immensely – I promise. The journey of self-development is very unique to each individual and needs the right amount of guidance, effort and knowledge to pull through to the other side. In fact, there is no other side as the journey is never ending with each new day bringing in more zeal and passion into our existence. But for this to happen our existing limiting beliefs, fears and mindsets have to be burnt and erased.

Instead of dragging one topic for the entirety of the book, I've cut into several topics in short bursts providing deep insights without compromising on quality or any extra fluff. As you procced through the book, you will gain deep understanding about the inner mechanics of the human ego and how to eliminate negativity from it's very root. You will also be provided with follow up exercises to help you to sustain those results. There is also a value assessment guide near the end of the book which I highly recommend you to commit to with utmost sincerity.

All the concepts explained in this book have been researched heavily for years by me and rehashed time and again with utmost care to help you gain deep insights into the issues in your life. The methods and exercises laid out have been tested by me and their efficiency being proven beyond doubt.

If you sincerely follow through with this book, I can assure you that it will leave a deep impact and bring about radical shifts in your personal growth. You wouldn't even have to look any further at other sources.

All the best!

CHAPTER ONE

IMPORTANCE OF AWARENESS

As a child there was one phrase which I was repeatedly told by my elders – Knowledge is power. They said, knowledge pulls you out of ignorance and gives you a chance to thrive in this world. But they never went deep enough to explain what 'knowledge' were they really referring to. Every time I would confront them with the question, they would say – just study, that's all you need to do right now. Sounded vague to me… whether it was my inability to intuitively grasp or their inability to explain, I could never really understand.

I left home at the age of 17 and went to another city to pursue my graduation. It was around this time that I was introduced to self-development. Thinking it would elevate my issues (I had many) coupled with my ever-curious mind, I jumped in. I took the generalist approach that is diving into several different philosophies, theories and disciplines which equipped me with a lot of knowledge. I spent hours, days and weeks breaking down concepts in my head, going out and debating them with my friends and writing my own notes which gave me immense clarity and insight. I started to think in systems and had radical shifts in perception that repeatedly challenged the way I interpreted the world. It made me more aware of my existence so to speak giving me a wholistic understanding of the world which kept expanding as time passed by.

That's when it dawned on me! The elders were right... but partially. It's true that knowledge is power but there was a missing link in that. Something that took me years to decode. The path from knowledge to power is not direct and is intercepted by awareness.

Knowledge – Awareness – Power

Knowledge gives rise to awareness. The intake of knowledge forms small of pockets of wisdom that after repeated rehashing comes out as awareness. Awareness cannot be articulated so to speak and has to be directly experienced by the individual. It is the knowing of one's own self at a very deep and intimate level. Awareness empowers one to transit from a state of confusion and hopelessness to a state of power. It is the ultimate catalyst in the journey self-discovery or let's say in the journey of uncovering your true self.

All lasting growth of any kind (be it business, emotions, family, career, hobbies etc) involves increasing awareness in one form or another. For majority of the people the biggest problem with awareness is the catch-22. They are unaware of the fact that they are unaware. This paves way for immense self deception and delusions that masquerade as reality.

"Man assumes that he knows himself. But man doesn't realise that he is a machine. Developing awareness takes long and hard work. You really need to appreciate how deeply asleep you are before you take up the quest for raising your awareness. Because you delude yourself into thinking that you're highly aware, you cannot even begin to fathom what kind of higher states of consciousness exist." – Pyotr Ouspenskii (Psychology of Man's possible evolution)

Awareness is the true knowing of your own existence. It is when every channel of observation and contemplation is directed inwards and the self stands naked on the ice. Nothing to hide, nothing to fear and nothing to deny... just pure being as it were. It is that moment of clarity when you realise that the external world has no role in creating your own turmoil and it is you alone who stands in your way. All the mental processes, deep seated fears, judgements, beliefs and expectations fall bare in front of you and start to dissolve. It is that state where the ego can no longer deceive you and the illusion of being a victim is shattered.

Allowing oneself to drown in the totality of this concept is the first step towards true freedom. The state of liberation that we all aspire to have – state of bliss.

"The first step towards change is awareness. The second is acceptance." – Nathaniel Branden

"Awareness is a key ingredient in success. If you have it, teach it. If you lack it, seek it." – Michael B Kitson

CHAPTER TWO

AWARENESS ALONE IS CURATIVE

We shall first explore how to autocorrect any unwanted habit, with the most powerful tool at our disposal – Awareness.

More action is not always the answer despite what you might hear in self-development circles. In fact, neurosis can be defined as the excessive use of will, force and action to try to change your own behaviours therefore leading to self-sabotaging patterns, where you try to change something. Part of you wants to change it and part of you resists changing it. Therefore, net result being you are kind of stuck, dead in the water, not getting the kind of results that you want in life, feeling guilty and bad about these negative behaviours in your life that you don't even want but then secretly you actually do want them, which is why they are still there in your life.

One of the best ways to approach this is to really experience a reframing regarding the idea of how any change is actually created in your life. I want to share a deep and powerful insight with you right now that can improve your life by orders of magnitude. As simple as it is, if you just start to apply it.

- Awareness alone is curative!

This means that you don't necessarily need to plan and work really hard to let go of unwanted behaviours. In fact, what it means is that any unhealthy behaviour that you have will autocorrect in time merely through the process of observation – which is what awareness is essentially being.

So, when you are trying to actively change some aspect of your life, let's say you want to quit smoking / over eating / want to become more confident / more responsible with your finances, quitting porn / video games / social media etc. you are usually looking out for an active solution to them. Well there is an interesting alternative to this, which is to take the light of your awareness and shine it on the problem, trusting that with sufficient awareness the problem will simply dissolve!

What's really powerful yet simple about this method is that it does not require you to do anything much. It is extremely versatile and is applicable to all the issues you currently have in your life and will have later in your life.

Now let us understand how this works. This is a very powerful principle in advanced self-development. I want to program this into your mind so whenever the problem occurs, you are equipped with more than sufficient resources to drive it away. It is not possible to engage in an unhealthy behaviour while you are fully conscious and aware during it.

Think about this actually - if you are trying to engage in unhealthy behaviour and you cannot seem to stop it, right? This principle is implying that the reason you cannot stop is because you are doing it without awareness. If you were to do it with full awareness, the behaviour could not be continued. It would have to stop on its own. Don't just take me on my word for it, try it out yourself! This is something you have to really test out to admire its efficiency.

Now there is a catch, for this to work it needs a constant awareness. A certain duration of awareness. You cannot be aware of it for just a second or a minute, you have to be aware of it throughout the whole duration.

Let's take an example - if you are smoking and that you are already aware that it is unhealthy but when you smoke you are not really fully aware of it. So, if you were to smoke without trying to change anything about how you are smoking or forcing yourself to stop, if you were just to smoke with full awareness, being fully conscious of every drag you inhale, over and over again, you would not actually be able to continue to put that cigarette in your mouth. At some point it would just hit you like a lightning bolt to the head like... "wait a minute, what am I doing?" And you would just put it down because the awareness would reveal the damage that this is doing to yourself to such an extent that you wouldn't be able to authentically / genuinely continue the behaviour. Although for this to happen you would need constant awareness. It is not enough to say, "oh yeah, I know smoking is bad for me" and then just continue to smoke unconsciously - that's not going to work.

The other catch here with the broader principle of awareness alone being curative is that awareness is not as easy as you think it is. You might think you got that handled, but no! you don't realize how little awareness you have actually got. Even though the principle is timeless just like the law of gravity, you need sufficient focussed awareness to actually follow through on it. This also requires patience. This doesn't work in five seconds and probably won't work for you in five minutes, it requires a constant application over a little period of time.

While doing the activity stay 100% in the present moment. Look at the scenario from a third person perspective but do not judge! That's the key - don't get judgemental about it and just observe as it is happening with full focus. Be fully conscious. When starting with, don't pass moral judgements on whether it is right or wrong, just do it but with a hyper focus on the present and notice how it makes you feel. Be fully aware of all the feelings it is triggering in your mind and physical body. If you do this time and again, you will become so aware of the absurdity of the situation, of how much damage you are causing yourself that you would not need to force or guilt trip yourself into not indulging in that act anymore.

One of things that you will begin to notice when you start practicing this principle is just how unaware you are in your ordinary life! Especially when you are doing these unwanted behaviours. Really, the only way you can engage in any unwanted behaviours is by not being aware. Usually there are mechanisms facilitating your unawareness. There are subsidiary things you do while doing something unhealthy to distract you from the fact that you are doing something unhealthy.

So when you sit down at the television watching your favourite show with the giant bowl of ice cream or your favourite greasy food, you get sucked into the tv show and you totally surrender your awareness. This is the only way you can do that - sitting through that highly unhealthy behaviour. If you sat there for two hours with the awareness of how much you are wasting your life / health and all the other things you could have been doing with that time, then it would have been too painful to continue the behaviour.

Start thinking where this happens in your life and how you could extrapolate this principle into that situation.

Now, a few pointers or potential mistakes you could make while applying this principle:

- You might assume that awareness is the same thing as logical knowing. It is not! So a smoker, logically knows that smoking is very unhealthy, but that doesn't really do anything, right? Awareness is a in the moment observation of what is happening. Knowing is something like a memory. You can know a fact in the back of your memory and maybe pull it out once a while. Awareness is, are you aware right now? And that is a skill. Know that you have something like an awareness muscle in your mind and this muscle is flexed every time you are being consistently aware. It can be trained and developed. It is very different from logic as very smart people can still have bad behaviours because smart doesn't count for very much here. The deep lying neurotic needs that you have, that are the sources of these unwanted behaviours can be eliminated by awareness alone.

- Being aware is not the same as moralising or passing judgements. Awareness is not suppression. Don't suppress your desires or even the bad or so called evil ones. Do not force yourself to resist but do it with full concentration on the present moment, breaking it down to milliseconds. Don't manipulate your behaviour or mind into stopping as soon as you can as it would result in you failing only after giving yourself a short burst of ego boost that you conquered an unwanted habit. When in reality it is still lingering in your sub conscious mind and waiting to attack at your next weaker moment.

- Awareness is a very passive behaviour. It is not forceful but rather very scientific. Say a scientist is observing birds and trying to describe accurately their mating pattern. The scientist wouldn't run up to the birds and forcefully make the birds mate with his hands. That would not only be absurd but contradict the scientific method itself. He would rather sit back and make himself totally invisible to the birds, so the birds could do their own thing while he records the whole situation. That's what I want you to do. I want you to record in your own mind of what is happening at every moment.

This method would be applicable in any area of your life, procrastination, shyness, anger, depression, drugs, laziness, anxiety, fear, OCD, you name it!

CHAPTER THREE

GAIN MASTERY OF YOUR EMOTIONS

"There is nothing, good or bad, but thinking makes it so." – William Shakespeare (Hamlet)

This is a very fundamental truth in personal development and a very powerful paradigm to live from. It is also the opposite paradigm from which most people operate. Most people think that the emotions they experience, their moods, their feelings are all dictated by external circumstances. When someone pays you a compliment or something good is happening in your life, you are feeling excited and in reverse if someone insults you or something bad happens in your life, you feel really negative, right?

Well, there is a whole inner mechanism to this and most of the people miss the key component here –

Awareness. It is not the environment but rather how you think about the environment that induces those emotions in you and this is something that is completely within your control, something that can be changed even when the external environment is against you. You can change how you are perceiving and interpreting it therefore gaining emotional mastery. You feel it's the external circumstances that are keeping you stuck in life but actually it's your emotions which are induced by your interpretation of external circumstances.

All though the above is tough to swallow there is no better way to gain emotional mastery. Be it therapy, medication, distraction or even spilling it all out to your close ones. Let me expose you to this radically different paradigm of approaching emotions.

A few years ago, during the end of my graduate school I was going through some deep emotional problems. I was working on it constantly by meditating and seeking self-help material. I really wanted to weed out these issues and not just throw them under the carpet but erase them permanently. During this time, I happened to buy one of Tony Robbin's self-help audio packages and I still remember that one part where he mentioned that our emotions are not caused by the external world but by us. Although I logically understood what Tony was saying, I could not wrap my head around the fact that I was the root cause of all my issues and triggered emotions. It was really tough for me to come to acceptance with this concept. I still thought that if I could get rid of those external situations then all my frustrations would be gone. As I kept increasing my awareness and building my own emotional intelligence, I started coming to terms with how true Tony was. Most people have a hard time even believing this.

Let me demonstrate this to you via some models. Right now, the model that you are operating in goes as the following.

Model one:

At one hand, you have an external circumstance - let us say you get a raise / promotion in your job that triggers a happy emotion in you, which is followed by some sought of action. Your emotion leads to action so maybe you are going to work a little harder now that you have a better pay. The initial high (or low – depending on the situation) propels you to push harder and makes you more competitive, therefore putting you in line for an even higher raise next year. This again feeds back in, creating more positive emotions in you. That's the cycle which goes on and on.

Model two:

The first model is actually faulty. The following is what is really going on if you are aware. Taking the same external circumstance - a raise, but when you first perceive this raise through your senses, you do not have an emotion, you have a thought! This is what most people miss - that one has thoughts which create an interpretation filter. So, the raw fact that you got a raise comes in and passes through your interpretation filter which happens very quickly and subconsciously and we are not even aware of the thoughts which are shaping that. Then it gets translated into an emotion. Now, these emotions seem like they are very natural and have directly stemmed from the external circumstance but you are not aware of that filter being generated by your thoughts. Then of course you take certain actions based on that emotion (this part of the model is correct), generating more similar circumstances therefore giving more fodder for the mill to interpret.

This layer of interpretation is the key to life because if you gain awareness of this filter or layer then there will seldom be any external circumstance that would hold you back in life thus making you truly fulfilled and happy from the inside. If you do not practice awareness of this filter, I can almost be certain that you will be bogged down by every difficult situation in your path therefore not being able to generate the type of results that you sincerely desire. You have got this amazing power which is almost like a superpower - to assign meanings and interpretation to every external circumstance that crosses your five senses but when you deny this power or surrender this power to someone else or an external circumstance, you leave it all up to chance or random luck as we may call it. This is what generates chaos in people's lives, leaving interpretations up to chance and being totally unaware of the actual internal process.

Let us understand this interpretation filter a little more. The external situation has no value or meaning to it, in itself. Your thoughts in the mind assign or peg a value to it therefore giving it a meaning. Since for most people these thoughts are unconscious they will assign an automatic meaning to it. Over time, this thought will get conditioned to the external circumstance that it is always getting pegged to therefore making it difficult to have an open mind and looking at situations from various other perspectives.

Till now we only took a positive situation, so let's take a negative one too. Say your partner has left you in midst of what you considered an amazing relationship. Now instead of getting a raise, you have got some sought of negative event, right? Wrong! It is not a negative event, it is just an event. It is the filter of interpretation that you are putting on it therefore assigning positive or negative value on it. So, if someone cheats on you and you are feeling bad about it, let's see what kind of thoughts are necessary to generate that emotion? "that arsehole broke my trust! We had such a good thing going and he/she burned it to the ground, I feel so betrayed… and on top of all this, how am I going to find another great lover, it was hard enough to find this one… and what if even they turn out to be such an arsehole, what if I die miserable and lonely." and the mental rant goes on. Well, if this is your chain of thought then of course you are going to feel bitter rage and misery. So, what kind of action will this create? It might not create any action at all. Being so depressed you are probably not going to date somebody else or start looking for another partner. You would probably withdraw in your shell and create walls around you being always suspicious and spiteful towards the opposite sex. Will this mindset lead you to finding a better partner? Probably no, it's actually going to shut off therefore reducing your chances to

- Their ego cannot accept this. Who wants to admit that they are causing their own suffering? The ego loves to play the blame game but the parody is, in doing so it is giving up all its potential control over the situation.

The key takeaway is that you need to take 100% responsibility for your emotions. Don't blame it on others or some situation. Nobody is causing you feel angry, jealous, loved or joy. You are causing it... always.

As practical application is of utmost importance, do this following exercise for the next seven days. Take a 100% responsibility for all your emotions, especially the negative ones. So, if you feel stressed, overwhelmed, lonely, angry, worry etc, I want you to stop and notice. When you are in the middle of that storm of emotions, pause and take note of the thoughts that you are creating right there in the moment. Then you will become aware of the thoughts that are governing your current emotions. Try to do that for seven days straight and see how differently you start viewing life. If you miss some, don't beat yourself over it as you have just started out and it will take a while. Not to mention how pleasantly surprised you would be to not have noticed this interpretation process ever in the past.

find your dream mate. Not only will you further isolate yourself but you will also get into further unsatisfactory relationships spearheaded by your negative mindset which will throw you in a downward spiral. The further circumstances will induce more negative emotions in you.

Now you might argue that this is all very logical but what if it happened for real, imagine yourself in that moment with your partner, what would you do? Wouldn't this logical principle go out of the window? Well, let's have a look. It's true that sometimes emotions trigger you but that does not mean that there is no filter there. You have still got the thought filter which is creating the negativity. Let's take this same scenario and approach it in a different perspective, where the only thing that changes is the thought filter. Now, instead of negative thinking, what if you thought something along the lines of... "you know I always had this gut feeling, that this person wasn't right for me, if I really love myself I am going to go out and date and what if I find someone who is an even better match for me? Why should I miss that? What if I can find someone who can completely accept me for what I am, what if he/she enjoys some things that I really do, what if I want to start a family with him/her who is probably right now searching for their perfect match too?" Notice how different these thoughts are and if you think them then how different is it going to make you feel? You can't help but feel optimistic. You are looking at this as a prospect of going out there and finding someone even better, you are looking at this scenario as an improvement to your life rather than something that would bog you down and beat you out. This will lead to optimism, excitement and anticipation of a better partner, a second chance given by life for you to make the most out of it, for you to be with someone who is your closest match. This will lead to action. You may go out and create an online dating profile, put more effort in your grooming, communication etc. Trying to be the best version of yourself therefore drastically enhances your chances of finding that dream lover. Not only will you come out of your older situation stronger but also much wiser, optimistic and thrilled to find your dream match.

So, in both the scenarios we have observed cycles that are either positive or negative. The question is, what kind of cycle are you creating for yourself? Now, do you realize that you are creating this cycle and it is not the cycle that is happening to you by itself.

"If you are distressed by anything external, the pain is not due to the thing itself but to your own estimate of it. In this you have the power to it, revoke at any moment." — *Marcus Aurelius (One of the greatest Roman emperors)*

Understand that you have the power to revoke your own estimate of things by being aware of your interpretation filter at any given time. So, in a situation that majority would consider negative, remember that you have the control to reinterpret that situation by pegging a different value to it so you can generate some resource emotions that will further induce you to take action in the right direction thus leading to more positive results. This is a choice that you have.

You might argue about why would you choose to think positive thoughts when feeling negative comes naturally to you at that time. As we discussed it does not come naturally rather we induce it and are conditioned to auto respond due to lack of awareness. Also, if you use a little bit of your intelligence and foresight, you will see what will happen down the road. You need to ask yourself – this negative thought will create negative emotions which will in turn create negative actions, so, do I want negative actions in my life? Do I have a choice right now that will decide further course of action or how things play out in the future? Oh, actually I do have a choice. I can see the implications of these negative thoughts and maybe now I should think twice before surrendering to these negative thoughts. I don't have to go with what simply feels natural or more conditioned. I want an amazing life and that is more important to me than accepting what is 'natural'.

That moment between interpreting the situation to feeling an emotion, if we can manage to pass it through our filter of awareness, we win no matter what. Making a good situation better, to diffusing a bad situation to neutral or even good depending on our awareness during those crucial moments. There is no need to gamble with the results you want in life when you have real control over them. Now, we cannot control each and everything, that's a delusion. But we can control more than 90% of them which is way more than we think we currently can. This is a very powerful mindset and very few people think this way - The wise, the noble and the awakened.

So, why do only a few people think this way? Why are the majority always reacting unconsciously to everything? Well, there are a few factors for this:

- The family they grew up in. Most families don't teach such in depth principles and nor does school or society give this to you.
- They don't contemplate deeply.
- They are too lazy and surrender to whatever feels natural without their intelligence or foresight kicking in.
- Nobody around them is practicing this.
- For all their lives, decades together, they have been operating from the first model thinking that they have no say over their emotions which makes them too hardwired to even see another better possibility.
- They lack self-honesty and self-awareness. Right now, they don't accept how little awareness they have and how much more they could have.

CHAPTER FOUR

DEALING WITH STRONG NEGATIVE EMOTIONS

In the previous chapter we delved into what emotions really are and how to gain mastery over our interpretation filter. We learnt how to divert ourselves from negativity and always have a brighter approach towards life. In this chapter we will be taking a slightly different approach to deal with strong negative emotions but none the less very effective. With the help of awareness not only can we withstand them but also delete them forever without harbouring any residual or full-fledged feeling for long durations. After I walk you through this, in the end you will understand that you can erase pain forever. What will be left behind will only be the memory of the situation, no emotions attached to because let's face it, the human mind does not forget things too easily. A memory just like any other regular memory but with little to no emotions hooked to it.

By strong negative emotions, I mean the entire spectrum, from sadness to hurt, loss, fear, crippling anxiety, rage, depression and everything that falls in between.

> *"The tendency to avoid emotional suffering is the cause of all mental illness. To lead a healthy spiritual life, we must face problems directly and experience the pain involved."*   - Scott P (Author of the book – The road less travelled)

The solution to deal with a strong negative emotion is very simple and that is to allow yourself to feel the emotion completely. As counter intuitive as it sounds, we seldom follow this road and never face our emotions head on. Hold on with me as I assume you might be a little perplexed right now. We never face our emotions head on because we do not want to let our guard down and become vulnerable. We think that when we allow ourselves to be vulnerable, it somehow makes us weak and puts us in harm's way. When in fact, it's actually the opposite of that. It's hard for the ego to see this at first and to accept that it should allow itself to feel the full impact of a strong negative emotion. All the ego wants to do is to resist, deny and run away trying to feel only pleasant and good by supressing the negative emotion. That's what the ego wants - to eat the candy and avoid the salad.

To start off with, we have to be okay with allowing ourselves to be vulnerable. It won't make you small or weak but rather the opposite of these. But you could argue, "why should I make myself vulnerable? If I'm vulnerable, won't I get hurt? Isn't that what has happened in the past?" In a way, you are partially correct according to what your psychology consists of, especially if you have a lot of problems in your life. The reasons you have all these problems right now in your professional life, relationship, family etc. is because in your childhood you received these wounds and you did open yourself up thus you were vulnerable. What followed was that you had to close yourself down because the hurt was so painful. The vulnerability was so painful that you then started erecting defences, various shields to protect yourself and you adopted certain vows telling yourself that you would never again allow yourself to be vulnerable with people or in an intimate relationship, career, finances or some other situation.

Sadly, what you do now is spend a lot of mental energy simply maintaining these defences. It seems like they protect you but actually a major part of becoming mature and emotionally healthy is to dismantle all those defences that you erected in your childhood and teenage years. Not only do they weigh you down but they also prevent you from being aligned with the truth. The truth is really our saviour here when it comes to emotions and if you are still uncertain of giving up your defences, here's the raw fact - What you do not admit to yourself right now is that you are actually vulnerable. It doesn't matter how many defences you have put up, you are still vulnerable.

Let me explain the above with an example I like to think of when I think about vulnerability. Imagine those macho tough guys, the guy who bench presses 300 pounds and is ripped to perfection. So, this guy is the macho guy or the 'invulnerable guy', oh he is surely not vulnerable. Well, as he is pressing his 300 pounds in the gym looking so macho carrying himself in the classic alpha male style, if I walked up to him with a gun and pointed it at his head… that's it, lights out for him. All the muscles in the world and all the alpha talks or poses cannot win against a bullet. It doesn't matter who you are but you are vulnerable. Be it the richest person in the world, the strongest or a military dictator surrounding himself with hundreds of body guards, it doesn't matter. In fact, the more you try to defend yourself, the more vulnerable you are. Let us, rationally admit to ourselves that we are in fact vulnerable and we can get hurt. It's a part of life, a part of being a human being.

Now, what do we do about this? Well, your job is not to play defence but become a super conductor. You see, regular house hold wires conduct current. Now current is conducted through a material and this material has a conductive property into it along with something called resistance. Resistance is the inherent nature of the material (metal) which resists the flow of current through it therefore heating up and after a certain point it could start to melt the wire. The reason I mentioned this is because it's a really good analogy as to what you want to do with your negative emotions. Instead of resisting them which you always do as it is the standard automatic ego reaction, you need to open yourself to the point that you become a super conductor. Super conductor is the material that allows current to pass through it with zero resistance for very long distances without losing even the smallest portion of electricity nor generating any heat as no resistance is created. The more you resist, the more you burn yourself out.

So, what is the automatic ego reaction?

- We first get it when we experience a sting of negative emotion.
- The ego doesn't want to open up and feel it fully and instead it wants to act stoic and cool, sometimes even denying the negative situation in the face of reality.
- It wants to distract with food, drugs, sex, music or some other momentary outlet.
- It wants to sweep it under the rug and neglect it, sometimes for years and decades together.
- Sometimes it tries to suck it up. The body tenses all its muscles and you literally hold the pain inside.
- The ego tries to control and manipulate. Rather than feeling it, it tries to come up with a scheme to change it or falsely rationalize its way out.

These ego reactions kill your ability to super conduct and builds heavy resistance. From that resistance gets created most of your suffering. The only time we get damaged is when we resist / hold back and not because we allow ourselves to feel it fully by being vulnerable.

But to become an emotional superconductor, our mind needs training and awareness. Therefore, let me walk you through a practical method of dealing with any negative emotion in your life that you want to work through:

- Conjure up whatever emotion you are trying to work with here. Here we shall assume hurt as an example but please take whatever destructive emotion is bothering you.

- Relax your body and get into the present moment right now. Not into fantasies of revenge or sorrow but the present 'now'.

- Connect with your body. Feel what that hurt or whatever negative emotion you are feeling, is. Don't think or imagine, just feel. Try to locate it. Where is it? It's right there in your body and nowhere else. Feel how it feels, is there a tingling sensation in your forehead? Pain, ache? A warm sensation or a cold sensation? Are your muscles expanding or tensing? Lower abdomen maybe? Hands, shoulders? Back? Where is it? What's the quality of it? Is it mild or severe? Is it tight or lose? Does it feel hollow and sad or tight and angry?

- Do not judge anything, rather just take notice and become aware of it in your body.

- Now, open yourself up to it and fully feel what is there and let it in completely.

- Do not resist it at all. Give yourself the permission to fully feel the emotion (for example if you have water flowing through a channel or an irrigation gate, you can now open the gates to allow the water to flow through in totality).

- Observe with curiosity of what's actually flowing through. Don't judge or label it. Don't get trapped in your thoughts or the situation / people pegged to your negative event. Get out of your mind and stay totally in the 'now'.

- Allow again! You are so used to resisting that you unconsciously shut the gates. Therefore, allow again! If the hurt is building up intensely, that's fine as it is a part of the process.

- Do nothing. Don't divert yourself with food, sex or whatever, just sit there and completely feel the emotion while doing nothing at all.

Don't let your mind wander from the hurt and definitely don't get lost in revenge fantasies.

When you get hit by a strong emotion, it usually comes in waves. It's like you get hurt for a while then it subsides for a bit, then you remember it a while later and it hurts again. So, every time a wave hits you, follow the process for however long the negative emotional spell lasts for you. Physically remove any defences or tension. Let your belly, fists and jaw go loose while remembering to breathe deeply all throughout.

It's just like a pressure cooker. Yes, you can hold in the steam, but for long? It will keep releasing all the pent-up steam time and again, bit by bit until you open the lid. And if you do not open the lid then you would suffer forever. Instead if you just release the lid and let all the steam blow out at once then the cooker no more has any pressure inside. That's exactly what it means to be an emotional super conductor.

Understand that by doing this you are facing reality and to deny reality you have to deny the present moment. The only way you can deny the present moment is to disassociate from your body by going into your mind. That's the only place you can go to escape reality.

Before concluding this chapter, I would like to tackle certain limiting beliefs about emotions that you might have:

Negative emotions are bad. Actually, there is no such thing as a negative or a bad emotion. Emotion is just a sensation coursing through some part of your body and usually there is also some mental phenomenon that comes with it in form of mental imagery or mental verbal labels. If you feel hurt, notice that the hurt itself is not bad, that's just the ego's judgement. Your habit of resisting emotions is very strongly ingrained in you since your childhood and the labelling is very unconscious. When you dislike anything (here a feeling) you automatically label it as bad, evil or negative and you immediately say 'no'. One thing you can do to develop real emotional maturity is to stop labelling them as good or bad. By doing so, you create a separation between the emotion and yourself and thus being automatically compelled to fight it.

You might argue that wouldn't it be dangerous to let yourself be fully open to negative emotions? What if you would push yourself in harm's way physically or mentally?   Well, no it wouldn't be dangerous, in fact the opposite would be dangerous. You see, a lightning rod getting struck by thousands of volts of current still remains intact and undamaged for a very long time. The reason is because it doesn't resist at all, just lets the current pass through. Had it resisted, it would have burnt and charred in the very first bolt itself. So, if you find an emotion causing you suffering, remember that you are resisting on some level. If you weren't resisting, there would be no suffering.

You probably came here looking for a magic pill and the definition of magic pill is avoiding emotional labour. There is no technique where you don't have to feel anything and yet be liberated from negative emotions. Yes, there are distractions which are very temporary and shallow to say the least. Emotional labour is required if you want to erase pain from its roots permanently and never have to look back at it again. After all, you have to do all the heavy lifting yourself.

CHAPTER FIVE

THE PERFECTIONIST PARADOX

(Anti mastery/Hyper critical, a bit too much?)

One of the biggest personal development realizations that I have had last year occurred for me when I was at an enlightenment retreat. We weren't really working on personal development but rather on enlightenment and meditation methods. The more you delve into self-discovery, a lot baggage and revelatory insights (ah...ha moments) come up for you which are really therapeutic. I got a big insight into how hyper critical I had always been, whether it's with people, physical objects or products, rules and it made me realize how deep rooted was my need for perfectionism. I also realized how perfectionism in itself is very destructive and why people often confuse 'mastery' with perfectionism.

Awareness plays a huge role in this and through that you can understand in all the subtle and sneaky ways in which your need for 'perfect everything' is one of your biggest hurdles in life. It is not an asset but rather a massive liability that you need to get rid of before further damage is done. Following are some of the destructive consequences of perfectionism:

- Perfectionism means to constantly being critical which saps your happiness. Almost by definition it means that you are either angry or unhappy with something or the other and continuously looking for faults.

- It also wastes mental energy throughout the day. I noticed myself, instead of thinking about my top priorities and goals I was thinking about all these shallow and petty knit picks here and there which always distracted me from the real big picture.

- If you want everything to be perfect especially right off the bat then you psyche yourself out in a lot of situations in life. Not only do you fail to complete projects, you even fail to start them because you want everything to be perfect at the starting point (perfect conditions) therefore causing you to procrastinate heavily.

Perfectionism is an anti-mastery mindset. Mastery means focussing on the process rather than simply being narrow minded on results. A perfectionist is totally opposite of a master because he always focuses solely on the results.

What exactly is perfectionism? I would define it as a neurotic unwillingness to accept reality. Sometimes even to such a degree that you are unwilling to accept the fact you are 'unwilling to accept reality'. Here comes in an interesting theory called the 'paradox of choice'. The modern society is filled with over hundreds of choices every day and our brain really isn't designed to cope with so many choices. Having an overabundance of choice seems good on a superficial level but research says our brains have limited decision-making power and once that is exhausted it takes us time to replenish it.

Usually there are two types of people who deal with excess decision making - the maximisers and the satisfiers. Let's say the two go to a store to buy a vacuum cleaner. We have got vacuum cleaners of different sizes, shapes, colours, price, electric watts, warrantees, brands, customer reviews, unique features etc.

The maximiser being kind of a perfectionist walks in declaring that he needs the best vacuum cleaner in the world and that too within the best value. Therefore, he wants to find the sweet spot out of the various permutations and combinations he can fathom up in that store. He actually thinks he will feel happy this way by buying the perfect awesome vacuum cleaner. Now, when the satisfier the walks in and sees so many choices he just picks a couple on his instincts, probably spends ten minutes narrowing down on one and then goes ahead to buy it as long as it vacuums the floor and doesn't break.

Now, you might think the maximisers are better because after all it's about getting the most, right? Why settle when there is a better option ahead? Well, this is not quite true. It might seem that being the maximize will get you the maximum of everything including happiness but that is not the case. The maximiser's mind is constantly looking for perfect and sometimes it does find it but a lot of times it doesn't find the perfect and when it doesn't, he gets frustrated, upset and unhappy. The maximiser will find faults with almost everything thereby making it almost impossible to sustain happiness as reality does not bend to anyone's whims and fancies. Maybe a week later while surfing the web, the maximize comes across a new ad for a better vacuum cleaner and therefore ruining his state of 'ideal perfectionism' because now he is stuck with something he considers 'imperfect'. The satisfiers would see the same ad but probably be okay with it as long as their vacuum cleaner is doing the job just fine.

The main difference between these two groups is acceptance. It can be quite an uphill task for me to convince to take up acceptance because a few years ago I was a perfectionist myself, the typical hardnosed guy who wouldn't settle for even a fraction less. But what I realized is that I would never be happy this way in life. The moment a goal is achieved I would feel a 'high' that would be extremely short lived due to my obsessive nature of finding more and more faults leading to another conquest for perfectionism.

Perfectionism is a sneaky form of procrastination! Most forms of procrastination are pretty obvious like distractions, laziness / lethargy but perfectionism is extremely self-deceptive in this. When you are hyper critical, that energy and time you are using to be hyper critical is time that you should be spending on working towards the bigger goals in your life. Moreover, perfectionists always hunt for perfect situations. Unless everything is not in the right place either mentally or in their physical surroundings it gets very difficult for them to focus on the job at hand. The need for perfection keeps making them procrastinate the work to sometime later when the conditions are 'perfect'. Perfectionists also use (rather abuse) criticism to avoid taking blame in their lives.

Now, you might argue that if you stop being a perfectionist, wouldn't your work suffer? Not just work but every area of your life where your perfectionism drove you to find your 'perfect kinds, family, spouse, friends, home, food...' The problem with this is that there is a big fat lie that you tell yourself here, which is 'perfectionism is excellence'. You try to equate the two but that's not what it really is.

Art is not done for the sake of perfectionism but rather for the joy... the joy of creating the thing that you are most passionate about. Any person who is trying to actualize their ambition and life purpose is an artist. An artist of life just like a regular artist who attempts to paint their mental imagery on to canvas, an artist of life paints their mental imagery on to life. A true artist gets joy and delight in the process of making their art. Think about how much more enjoyable and productive your life would be if you truly got joy out of the entire process including the mistakes or imperfections. To be a real artist of life you need to focus your mind on mastery, that is the process - the full journey and not be obsessed with the outcome. The perfectionist is so outcome obsessed that mastery process itself gets corrupted. A masterful artist loves the art and directs every available resource towards mastering the journey - the results follow inevitably. Understand that both, criticizing others and criticising oneself are basically identical, like two sides of the same coin.

Think of the analogy of a sports car going at 150 miles an hour but with the parking brakes on. That's exactly how perfectionists function, not realizing that they are the ones holding themselves back. The paradox being that they are the ones causing maximum 'imperfection' in their hunt for perfection. Perhaps your perfectionism has served you good so far but I'm talking about the next level here. Imagine how much better would you do if the parking brake wasn't on. It would unleash your full potential.

CHAPTER SIX

HARNESS YOUR INTUITION

"The intuitive mind is a sacred gift and the rational mind a faithful servant. We have created a society that honours the servant and has forgotten the gift."

"I believe in intuition and inspiration. At times, I feel certain I am right while not knowing the reason."

"The only real valuable thing is intuition."

"The intellect has little to do on the road to discovery. There comes a leap in consciousness, call it intuition or what you will, the solution comes to you and you don't know how or why."

- *Sir Albert Einstein (all the above)*

Most people's lives lack big picture thinking, motivation and strategy. They get lost in life trying to fry the small fish when they should be chasing the big fish and therefore getting a lot less out of life than they could. This is especially bad in our modern society which is biased towards left brain thinking. We don't necessarily teach our children how to harness their intuition and nor do we hold it as acceptable for adults in this culture to use intuition for decision making. Think about this, if you are sitting in a top corporate boardroom proposing a business plan, they will ask you for an in detail logical explanation for every step but they will not accept any hunches or gut feelings. This is because in our culture everything has to be over rationalized and scrutinized but if you take a look at what's really going on, most of most important decisions you have made in your life have stemmed from your intuition. Then when you try to get your logical mind in there by rationalizing and over justifying it, it messes up the process. The extent to which you follow your intuition shapes the quality of your life because intuition is more powerful than logic will ever be. Notice, it is always the vision that comes first (be it the corporate boardroom or any area of your life) and then the logical mind fills in all the details.

The linear thinking that we have been conditioned to (cause and effect, from a to b to c…) is not able to crunch a lot of data. To have wisdom and make really high quality decisions you need to be able to crunch tonnes of data which the logical mind will never ever be able to grapple with. You need to trust your sub conscious mind to do these processes for you and your subconscious mind is not very logical, reasonable or linear. It's more like a vast distributed network that functions in truly mysterious ways but what it can do very consistently is crunch tonnes of data and very subtle factors that your logical mind would never understand. After crunching, it would come back to you with ideas, wisdom, insights and so forth in a very spontaneous way. Be careful not to discount intuition as some woo-woo airy fairy concept… it's really not, you just need to get in touch with it. It is more like a higher form of intelligence, like using a simple calculator vs using a vast super computer that functions in way that you don't even understand yet. What makes humans so amazing is our intuitive intelligence and not our logical intelligence.

When you silence your mind, and sit alone in solitude, you will notice that there's a little voice that comes up with all sorts of interesting things which different from our monkey mind and logic. Sought of like your higher self or your muse speaking to you. The catch is that intuition is difficult to follow and not as easy you might think.

There are few key failure points observed while people try to follow their intuition and their solutions:

1. Most people can't even hear it because it gets drowned out by culture, society and heavy influence of the people in their lives. Also, considering that our modern society mostly favours logical left brain thinking and has a bias towards being overly materialistic and overly pragmatic.

    Solution:

- The solution to this would be to acknowledge that true intelligence comes from something much deeper than your conscious mind.

- Another way would be to reduce distractions. Most people are so bogged down by obligations and constant sensory stimulation that they don't have even ten minutes a day for silence and solitude therefore failing to hear their own inner voice.

- Another powerful way to realize your intuition is to contemplate your own death. You need to realize that your life will not go on forever and that this materialistic orgy will fade away before the universe taken another breathe. When you get a grasp of this, your priorities will start to realign. If you ever read about people having near death experiences (be it cancer, car crash, military etc), you would know that all their priorities get reshuffled because they came face to face with death. When you are faced with death, materialistic distractions and logic stop being significant to you.

- Meditation is one of the most powerful tools you can use to enhance your intuition. The more you meditate, the more attuned you will become to that subtle muse voice inside of you.

- You need to also be more attuned to your emotions. Feel your emotions more fully in a holistic manner to pave way for your intuition to surface.

2. Even when people are able to hear their intuition, they are so full of personal impurities that they cannot follow it. The problem is you have got this big ego, various cravings, fears, traumas and dogmas which are all a distorting filter over your intuition. The bigger your ego, the more distorted and corrupted your intuition will be.

Solution:

- To have benevolent motives in your life and make sure that whatever you are moving towards in life is coming from deep seated passion and not from defensiveness, fear, craving or protecting your self-proclaimed dogmas. Notice how different all of these are than coming from deep rooted passion.

- Keep higher and more noble goals which are less about yourself and more about the people around you and the benefit of the world at large. When you got things like craving for approval, lust and cheap thrills then you cannot truly surrender to your higher intelligence because the intuition will try to push you beyond all that but you won't be able to go there as you are weighed down by all these heavy egoic things.

- Change your environment. Not only are there constant impurities in the modern world but also, it's like an impurity generating machine. It recreates impurities in such a way that the moment you remove some impurities it fills them right back in even more. It's like garbage in, garbage out. Disassociate yourself from unhealthy people, stop consuming low value information and most importantly go out into the nature more often.

- Ensure that you free your body of tension. Intuition doesn't just demand mental clarity but also physiological wellbeing. Get some exercise, yoga or massage done along with correct breathing technique. One of the best ways to eradicate tension immediately from your body is box breathing, which was first talked about by the duo navy seals who wrote the book 'extreme ownership'. It helped the Seal survive an excruciating mission underwater with little hope of survival. All you need to do is inhale deeply for five seconds, hold the breath in for next five seconds, then exhale for another five seconds and finally hold for five more seconds before inhaling again. It's very simple but supremely effective. Repeating this twenty second cycle for a few minutes will instantly release physiological tension. As the old saying goes, the body follows the mind and the mind follows the body, releasing physiological tension will also pave way for mental clarity to follow.

3. The third failure point is even when some people have intuitive hits, they ignore it. Even when they recognize that their intuition is trying to guide them, they reject it and instead rely on the obvious that is right in front of them as a guide. The problem here is twofold. One is lack of proper commitment to your intuition and the second is lack of requisite variety or flexibility in being able to get something accomplished.

Solution:

- You need to realize that your number one job is to serve your intuition. Your intuition knows exactly what you are, what are your deepest desires and where do you want to be in the end of your life. Your job is to trust it and execute its instructions with due diligence.
- You need to commit to following your intuition because following it takes courage, discipline and work. It can be especially challenging if you have ignored it and followed simple obvious sensory inputs all your life.

- You must create a sort of intuition incubator in your life. You need to incubate the intuitions because they don't come to you in a polished, precise and step by step blueprint form.

- Start journaling your intuitions, both small and big ones. Track them down, articulate them in specific language, contemplate on them and then create action plans starting out with the smaller ones first.

- Be very strategic of how you go about actualizing your intuition as some may take years of ground work to lay down the foundation for it to bear fruit.

How do we tell apart, true vs false intuitions?

Sometimes we may get an intuition but we are not quite sure if it is coming from the right place or it could be the ego being sneaky and deceptive. This is quite simple to filter out. False intuitions defend themselves with justifications when they are questioned whereas true intuitions are silent when they are questioned yet the more you question them, they still continue to have that magnetic pull to them.

So, if you have an intuition, go ahead and question it. I'm not asking you to blindly follow whatever random impulse your gut may be throwing at you. Therefore, sit with it, ponder over it, question it and while questioning it be very mindful about what happens. If you get rational answers then it's probably your ego masquerading as your intuition. If it has that silent pull towards it, does not give any replies, does not try to reason with you and yet has a strong impression then it's your true intuition and you must follow it. Also, the false intuition tends to be kind of protective, coming from a place of playing not to lose or to escape and avoid something. Whereas, the true intuition tends to be aspirational, coming from a place of beauty and it's playing to win. Majority of the people often confuse their ego with intuition and end up taking wrong decisions therefore swearing to never follow their gut again. Don't fall into the same trap of missing out on of the biggest gifts to mankind.

"Don't let the noise of other people's opinions drown out your own inner voice."

"Have the courage to follow your heart and intuition. They somehow know what you truly want to become."

"Intuition is a very powerful thing, more powerful than intellect, in my opinion."

-   *Steve Jobs (all the above)*

CHAPTER SEVEN

CREATING RESULTS THROUGH AWARENESS

One thing I noticed in most of the people around me is that they are especially bad at generating results. The world runs on results, whether it's business, money, career, fitness or even our internal mood are results. Result making is an attitude or approach that you take towards life. Unleashing your potential entails getting results. Most people get lost in ideas and theories about how they going to make some significant change or shift in their life or achieve a set goal. These theories have no value unless you know how to translate them into the real world and doing so is an ability, something that you need to train yourself to do.

You see, society has set us into a mode of complacence. You can just follow the masses the lead a passive life whose quality degrades as time passes by. Life is pretty easy these days as compared to what it used to be, let's say 10,000 years ago… at that time it was either get results or die!

An interesting dynamic of why people are not good result makers is because they don't hold their own feet to the fire of reality. What I noticed in myself when I was younger was that I used to get these really cool ideas regarding some small start-up, comics, university festivals, new system implementations and so on but they used to just remain as dreams. They were like my personal fantasy bubbles which somehow weren't getting grounded to reality. But as I got older, reality started kicking in… I had to find myself a job to pay bills and start keeping up a lot of routines in order to keep my existence intact. So, when the rubber met the road it was almost like, 'oh my dreams are gone now, they would never come into fruition' and things felt like such a lockdown. When the bubble touches the edge of reality it bursts because the bubble is usually not strong enough. Now it's a scramble and an uphill battle of trying to rearrange and integrate our dreams into reality more often than not compromising on the quality. It's also very emotionally taxing for us to have our bubbles popped.

So, the grounding process of our dreams is not just a onetime thing. We have to do it again and again and this is the secret of a really good results maker. They willingly and wilfully indulge in the translation process of dreams into reality which is usually very messy, tiresome, emotionally draining and uphill. Reality doesn't change for you, you've got to change for reality.

Here you are presented with two options. The first one being the emotionally easy one of discarding your dreams and staying in your little zone. It's easy and requires no work other than a bit of regret and self-loathing. The second option however is the more emotionally difficult and often the mature one. You go back to the drawing board and think something along the lines of, 'man, I was really misguided about my understanding of reality. I thought this project would fly, but it's not going to... not even close! Let me restructure my whole dream and also introspect and analyse my own internal process. What kind of beliefs do I hold about the world which are making it impossible for me to get this project off the ground in the real world?'. This process forces you to mature, evolve and let go of old dogmas about the way you think things should work. You have to be humble enough to let reality work on you and this is what I call holding your feet to the fire of reality.

Guess what? This is applicable to any field in your life including relationships and emotional wellbeing too. It's one thing to dream of having a loving relationship and another thing to actually have it, to engineer and design it the way you dreamt of in a concrete and sustainable fashion. It doesn't just happen by accident and rather takes a lot of skill and effort to bring it into fruition.

Even when people do take concrete steps they get stuck in these loops where the results are minimal therefore missing a major link that their actions have to aligned to the goal and current scenario alike. They have to adapt and be ready to change their course of action without being too hung up with old methods and traditions.

Here is how a results maker thinks:

-   You have to actually value tangible results. This is a mindset and an attitude shift. For example, if you're an employer and your employees are coming to you with stuff they are supposed to be doing (but they aren't getting the desired results), you have to be the one that actually sets the standards for tangible results to be created. Are you holding yourself to that high standard of 'I have to create tangible results otherwise I am not really doing anything'?

-   You actually have to create stuff. Now this seems a bit over simplified but it's necessary to ask yourself 'are you a creator in your life?'. For me, I am creatively and project minded. What this means is that I see my life as a series of projects that I am working on and I find that this is a very useful mindset for creating results.

-   Do you understand what does a project mean? A project is a projection of your ideas and dreams onto reality. Reality is the screen and your actions are the projector. But if the projector is not even switched on how will anything appear on the screen? How do you want to live your life? Do you want to let reality drag you around or do you want to project your dreams and shape your surroundings in a concrete fashion?

- Desire to impact people. Believe it or not, this is huge. People play a massive role in your external reality and you cannot deny that. Any projection onto reality will have a direct impact on the people around you or at large. Every projection has an impact on the world and shapes it. Our world is in an ever fluid state getting shaped by millions of concrete projections every day. Whether it's creating a piece of art to writing a new content to designing new systems to starting a new business or anything that has even the tiniest ability to mould external reality. External reality won't change just with your thoughts and inner world play. Some people don't care about impacting people and all they want is a cushy life. If that's you, you are going to be terrible at creating results.

- Talk is cheap. People love theorizing new possibilities of various projects that they wish to start mentally detailing every step of it but not realizing any of them in the end of the day.

The real deal is in already starting off my taking some concrete actions. Sure, you can spend time on planning but action has to go hand in hand with planning from the very first moment itself. These days whenever someone tells me that they are going to do something, in my mind it's nothing… just empty sounds. If you want to really do something, don't tell you're going to do it (this way, that way etc) just go and do it! Start with action, break that bubble of inertia. Often times talk is just a distraction from holding your feet to the fire therefore keeping you in your little safe zone and giving you a false illusory satisfaction of getting something done when the truth couldn't be any further from it.

- Work for excellence. Value excellence for its own sake and always put out the very best you can.

- Take personal responsibility for making it happen. No matter what the project is, you have to believe that it is your job and nobody else is going to do it for you and nor will they be held responsible. Stop waiting for someday else to lead you, show you the way or tell you what to do. It's you who has to take the first initiative at all costs.

- Working the big picture. A results maker is powerful because he has a wholistic understanding of why we he is working and where exactly is it heading. The crucial component here being the purpose behind his actions. Picture yourself being able to see your whole project and its potential direction and impact from a 1,000 feet elevation. How would a certain course of action path and how would it connect to the long-term vision laid out? Being able to observe the whole web in its entirety rather than getting lost in the narrow by lanes.

- You have to build a strong work ethic and that's something which is really lacking these days amongst the masses. Due to the way modern society is designed and as kids we have been spoon-fed to a large extent from free entertainment to sheltered living, the work ethics have been diluted and this translates into adulthood as mediocrity. It's difficult to build dedicated work ethics especially in a culture that is bent upon making you dependent and laid back, so one might have to go against the grain on this one.

- Must be willing to use brute force. If you can see that there's a result you could potentially get to by brute forcing or hustling your way very hard through work then by all means go for it. Don't be passive, reluctant or procrastinate as that will only stack the odds further against you. Don't search for magic solutions… if you have to sit for 12 hours at a stretch and hammer your way through the work to accomplish a potential goal in sight then don't let lethargy get in the way. This doesn't mean you have to do menial labour and totally obsess over perfection. But if you can see that a burst of work can boost you to the next level then there's no reason why you shouldn't go for it.

- Be willing to sacrifice comfort. This is probably the most crucial of all and yet we put it on the back seat so often. Maybe you've to skip your next vacation or stay up all night to get certain work done in a specified time frame or learn a new skill before next fall… all in order to advance yourself. So are you willing to do those or are you choosing temporary comfort over heavy benefit / potential advancement? We all know that counter intuitively hedonism doesn't produce much happiness in the long run. So, watch out for that.

- You have to be willing to change yourself to get the result. You cannot stay at a rigid place and expect reality around you to rearrange as per your whims and fancies. With every project that needs to implemented / achieved, you have to be willing to let go a part of your older self and forge into someone more dynamic and adaptable. Every external shift causes an internal shift, no matter however small and whether you realise it or not. So, in order to make a big external shift, be prepared to have an internal change in degree at least equal if not more as compared to the external. Most people are not willing to do this. They will go as far as reaching the edge of their comfort zones and fall back, being tricked into falsely believing that they have maxed themselves out when in fact the game has barely even begun. If a results maker notices that his goal post is let's say 5 steps above his current comfort zone then he would transform his entire psyche and work ethic in order to get to the goal post. He would rearrange his internal state in order to rearrange his external environment. Whatever it takes, maybe research, coaching, seminars, practicing, studying anything... to get to the next goal post. In fact, these things are basic mandatory needs for any decent goal and you might have to get heavy technical skills in your department to make that jump beyond your current comfort zone. Going a step further would be dropping entire chunks of belief systems and world views. Most people would not even understand why such deep psychological changes are needed to rearrange external reality but it's highly interconnected at a meta level. For example, if you are a very dogmatic person and having trouble being radically open minded then you are going to face quite a bit of resistance in generating solid results. If you align yourself with reality no matter what the emotional cost is then the results are bound to follow through. Notice I am not talking about ignoring emotions here but sacrificing temporary sentiments for long term fulfilment. Trying to preserve your ego even in the face of harsh reality is plain retarded and probably the most stupid decision.

- Throw yourself into demanding situations. To elaborate on the point above, there is nothing more rewarding than launching yourself out of your comfort zone. For example, take a military boot camp where you enrol a soft new recruit, throw them into a couple of months of brutal training and in the end, they come out as tough as nails. What happens there is that their psyche just gets shell shocked into transforming. Some people can't handle it and end up breaking down but those who do survive it come out much stronger than they could ever fathom. So, if you've been living in that small comfort zone of yours for years together how about throwing yourself into a demanding situation?

- Be around exceptional people. If you surround yourself with mediocre people who are not generating any results in life then you will assimilate their attitudes and mindsets thus believing that, that's normal.

- Starting your own venture / business. This is already slightly touched upon above but I think nothing holds your feet to the fire more than starting your own business and seeing the harsh, cutthroat and brutal realities of the market place.

- Train yourself to like the burn. In a semi masochistic way, train yourself to love the harshness. During the Navy Seal training, the candidates are made to fall in love with pain. They crave pain and thrive in the face of it. When pain kicks in, all the mediocre ones stop dead on their tracks but for the navy seal the party has just begun. Of course, you don't have to take it this far but drawing some inspiration from them can help you go long way.

CHAPTER EIGHT

STOP JUDGING YOURSELF (And others)

The problem is that judgements are poisoning your life and you're usually not aware of how this mechanism works on a deeper level. When you judge others, you don't realise that you are also judging yourself at the same time therefore being unaware of how judgement backfires.
 I wish to deep dive on the following: Judgements that you make of others always apply to you – this gives you the understanding to uproot this toxic habit from its core.

Let's take the example of judging fat people. Maybe you are one of those people who values his or her health, goes to the gym, works out and eats healthy but you probably judge fat people as they are walking down the street. Maybe you and your friends sometimes laugh at fat people because you all are into fitness stuff. Okay, fair enough… but here's the problem with this. (To understand the backfire, we shall take another tangential example in an attempt to integrate it with the former and give a larger perspective).

Say you go to your relative's home for thanksgiving and it's a big feast with people completely indulging into heavy caloric meals. So, you start to indulge little bit, fall off your healthy diet and start to put on maybe an inch or two around your waist. All of a sudden, your belt's getting a little tighter and you probably have to loosen up the notch by one. This induces a bit of negative feeling inside you, probably some shame or a dent in self-esteem. But why does it induce really? Because you have been judging fat people for years. Now, of course, you aren't fat but even as you begin to creep towards fatness, you start getting neurotic about it. So, you begin the self-talk as "okay I got to get back at the gym and hit it really hard to get back in my former shape". Now, your whole fitness routine becomes like this avoidance and escape of coming under the effect of your own past judgements thus becoming a terrible motivation of going to the gym. This one example explores one of the many possibilities of how a backfired judgement could manifest.

Stretching the same example, let's say in the future your partner starts gaining a few pounds.

This bothers you but you do not know how to express it to them directly… maybe it would offend them, so you resist it for a while. But soon, the built-up tension is released in arguments over other issues (as a mask for its root which is: them gaining weight has impounded your self-esteem but it cannot directly be expressed, so the steam is let out in other directions).

Another example, have you ever judged rich people? Like you see someone driving a Mercedes or a Ferrari down the street or sitting in a fancy restaurant with a Rolex as you are walking down by the street corner. And you think to yourself, "oh man, that's such a rich do*c*ebag, sitting there eating his rich lunch, wining and dining with his rich girlfriend and his rich car, how materialistic… I bet you he is some wall street broker type of guy, who swindled some old grand lady out of her retirement savings." So, you come up with that kind of story and you do this over and over again. Maybe you grew up in a middle-class family where your parents made these kinds of judgements about rich people. Such kinds of judgements were also reinforced by your friends who probably were middle class too.

Now, as an adult maybe this is how it backfires on you - You are thinking of starting your own business, but your mind still hasn't made that leap or space for a nice, rich person as it automatically classified all rich people as d-bags therefore getting burnt by your own judgements. Maybe this sub consciously leads you to sabotage your own business or if you're thinking of going into business, you just let go of that dream.

This is what you need to understand: All this happens very sub consciously and you are not directly aware of it happening. It's not clear to you in your mind when you sabotage your own business / relationship / gym routine that it's coming from a judgement you made and solidified 5/10/20 years earlier. The connection is very blurry but if you connect all the dots you will start to see the truth of it and yes, it's very subtle.

Another example and my personal favourite of the lot! Let's say you are a regular gym goer who has been lifting for a couple of years and knows the inside out of fitness with all the routines, procedures etc. So, when a newbie comes in especially all the fresh green horns on the 1st of January, you are your buddies are constantly judging how noob-ish they are and how almost all their exercises do not coincide with the 'correct way'. But then when you yourself go on to learn a new skill in the future and most probably suck at it in the beginning, it eats you from the core with all the people watching and constant inefficiency / failure and anxiety, leading you to probably quit the skill soon.

The following will be an example of a positive judgement backfiring. Let's say you have a guy at your office whom you really admire. He has a great personality, confidence, charismatic, charming, outgoing etc. And now you start to feel like you are inadequate because you judged him as being up there and yourself below him. Maybe you are shyer, reserved and introverted and you don't understand how it seems so effortless for him.
So, some years later although you are still speaking to people in your office etc, you are feeling inadequate because of the judgement that you had formed and solidified five years ago.

In a sense, judging is like creating a law or a loop which your mind stores and it hence forth starts getting applied to all your future situations because the mind tries to maintain consistency and integrity with itself.

For you, these examples might be totally different but I wanted to use them to get your mind jogging and start attempting to connect all the dots to trace it back down. The fundamental problem in all these examples is that you are disowning a part of reality. You are creating these rigid rules (which actually are totally arbitrary) which come back to enslave you. You feel a heavy obligation to stay consistent with all your past judgements and cannot admit to being wrong therefore blocking off a lot of avenues within reality. This seals your fate thus making you inflexible in life and crippling spontaneity and worst of all? you are not even aware of this mechanism playing in the background. You keep asking yourself, "why do I feel shame all the time? Why do I feel guilty all the time? Why do I feel unsatisfied all the time?" and so on, all along only scratching the surface without connecting all the dots.

Here is a practical exercise for you, to help you with this subject:

- Make a giant list about every single judgement you've ever made about other people (as far as your memory recalls or at least all the reasonably significant, impressionable events /

people in your life. The larger the list, the better!).

- Now, write down every judgement you have ever made about yourself as a separate list.

- While doing this you want to get into a stream of consciousness where you let it just pour out of you. Might take you 30 minutes to sit there and fill the list up without any filtering. Write down even the most evil, vile and harshest judgements you have ever made. Put down both negatives and positives, if you judged someone to be a complete a**hole or you put someone on the pedestal.

- Now, mark out the judgements that you think have a stronger potential to backfire on you or to create neurotic patterns in your life. How do you know which ones to select? Well, they kind of just jump... try using your gut instinct.

- Remember to get everything out of your system. This is not the time to be nice or politically correct.

So, in a nutshell to stop judging other people you need to first stop judging yourself. Your judgements only reflect your own inner fears and insecurities. Hopefully you can now see the dynamic where it's a double-edged sword cutting both ways, inside and outside.

So, how do you begin to put the brakes?

- Be very mindful and aware of how you judge other people. Judgements are usually subtler than we think and are not usually black or white.

- Remember you judge a lot more than you think and it takes a period of increased awareness to start to see this.

- Be more mindful of how your judgements are damaging you. So, every time you see how they cut at another person, remind yourself to look at the other side too, i.e. inwards. Notice for example, that when you judge fat people it makes you more insecure about your own weight therefore getting trapped deeper into rigid arbitrary judgements.

CHAPTER NINE

SELF ACCEPTANCE

(How to stop beating yourself up)

This is a very counter intuitive thing because we don't allow ourselves to accept ourselves. This is one of the softer sides of self-development and usually a lot of us neglect it as self-development is sometimes falsely identified with add-ons like more success, confidence etc. when you initially begin practicing radical self-acceptance, it might come off as fruity or containing all the things that you 'don't want'. This is something I would strongly urge you to reconsider because it has the potential to produce massive results in your life. A sincere practice of self-acceptance can give you more results than the other self-help guides combined and I'm going to walk you through just that with a guided visualisation.

The real results that count are the inner results and that is what self-acceptance really goes to the core of. We are not trying to solve your mood problems or neurosis here through some sort of external fix or behavioural change. Sure, that stuff has its place but they are futile without genuine self-acceptance. Just going inside, yourself and looking that aspects of yourself that you have been denying for years and decades, opening them up and getting the shadow self to reintegrate is very important. In fact, your self-growth journey is just a façade if you do not do this. We all have a shadow self which we avoid confronting at all costs. All the darkness and negativity locked up in the Pandora's box never to be opened again, not realising how that bottling up and locking away is destroying our current self. When we hide them, and lock them away it literally makes us disintegrated. Disintegration means you are broken up and fragmented into multiple parts.

There is this aspect of you that wants to go to work and give your best but then there is also another aspect of you that wants to simply lay in bed. This is just one example of how conflicting forces work upon a single event creating distortion within you. You might be able to temporarily suppress one of them but the bandage soon falls off and the loop begins all over again. To become a calm, grounded and well-rounded individual, you have to learn to integrate all these different aspects and them into a state of complete harmony. If you're looking for an action plan to brute force your way through this, you are probably fishing in the wrong river. This needs more of an open surrender.

The most counter intuitive part here is, if you want to really self-accept then instead of hating your sins /

shadows, love them… love them to death. And yes, I agree with gives off a very fruity vibe at first but once you start doing it more and more, you realise how great it works. One common objection that would come up here would be, "well if I just accept myself as I am, if I accept my lazy/bad/destructive side then what is there to develop?". So, this is kind of the paradox of self-acceptance vs achievement and self-development. You really need to do both at the same time and I'm not telling you to accept yourself and then do nothing. I'm telling you to first accept yourself (first of all the act of self-acceptance is in itself a doing and it is something that you probably haven't been doing) and then go on and achieve the best you can.

The point is, only when you truly self-accept, do you begin to tap into authentic motivation. A lot of people are motivated by inauthentic motivations, which means if you hate an aspect of yourself… you use that to fuel your actions. For example, you hate your current looks so you go to the gym or you hate the fact that you never have enough in your bank account so you go and work really hard. That's a very crude form of motivation / self-development. It works when that's all you've got, but eventually you have to evolve past that and get to the higher levels.

The following will be a guided visualisation, which you can do as you read this or read it first and do it later with closed eyes. Although, the later would be more effective. This will be worth your time, I promise. Sit still and comfortably throughout the duration of this visualisation and spend some time on each step.

- Get in the present moment. Become aware of the feelings in your body. Get aware of your thoughts and breathing. Go nice and slow at your own pace. Get very focussed and centred of what's happening in the present moment right now.

- Notice that right now as you're sitting there, bring to mind a strong feeling of love that you've ever experienced for something. (Could be anything from nature, videogames, sex, food, person... doesn't matter)

- Now, isolate that feeling of love so that there is just this cloud of love that you're feeling independent of thing itself (which you thought off to trigger the love). Feel that love in your mind, heart and anywhere else that you would feel it in your body.

- I now want you to apply that love, to the one that you are right now who is sitting there in the present moment. Don't ask, "how do I do this?", just do it. Just give yourself love right now, unconditionally for no reason whatsoever. Do not look for justifications or rationalisations.

- Now bring to mind, this one that's you, who gets angry sometimes. Now, give that one love. Give the angry part of you love, just infuse it with love without asking how or why.

- Now bring to mind, this one who is sitting there, has been treated unfairly in the past. Haven't you been treated unfairly before? And felt bad about it... now give that one love. Put love on the wound.

- Now bring to mind, this one who is sitting there, has treated other people unfairly. Haven't you wounded other people? The one who has wounded others, bring that one to mind and give that one your love.

- Now bring to mind, this one who is sitting there, has been critical to others. The part of you that is critical and judgemental all the time. Give it love.

- At this point, if you notice resistance to giving love, just give that resistance love and let it dissolve.

- Now bring to mind, this one who is sitting there, who has had struggles with money. Maybe you have in the past or maybe you still do. Bring that part to mind and give it love. Love that part of you, which is bad with money.

- Now bring to mind, this one who is sitting there, has suffered embarrassment. Give it love. Show it compassion and understanding. Fully accept it as though it was your child or a beloved pet.

- Now bring to mind, this one who is sitting there, who has made mistakes. Isn't there a part of you that makes mistakes and screws up in life? Bring it up and give it your unconditional love and understanding without any reservations.

- Now bring to mind, this one who is sitting there, who acts lazy and likes to procrastinate. I want you to give it your full unconditional love. Infuse it with your understanding and compassion.

- Now bring to mind, this one who is sitting there, who is afraid and anxious. Give that one unconditional love and compassion.

- Now bring to mind, this one who is sitting there, who hates his / her physical appearance.

Give that part all of your love, understanding and compassion.

- Now bring to mind, this one who is sitting there, who feels lost in life and doesn't quite know what to do. This part that doesn't have all the answers or directions it wants. That's confused and uncertain. Give that part your love, understanding and compassion.

- Now bring to mind, this one who is sitting there who feels sexually frustrated. Give that part of you, your unconditional love, understanding and compassion.

- Now bring to mind, this one who is sitting there, who has career problems and struggles at work / business / studies. Give that one your unconditional love, understanding and compassion.

- Now bring to mind, this one who has relationship problems. Give it unconditional love and understanding. Relationships are messy and complicated things.

- Now bring to mind, this one who is sitting there, who has family problems. Give that one your unconditional love and full understanding.

- Now bring to mind, this one who is sitting there, who has addictions and bad habits. Give that one your full love and compassion.

- Now bring to mind, this one who is sitting there, who lacks confidence and feels shy around other people. Give that one your love and compassion.

- Now bring to mind, this one who is sitting there, who has bad luck or misfortune. Like random undeserved bad luck and stuff happening to you in your life. Give that part of you, that hates bad luck, your love and compassion.

- Now bring to mind, this one who is sitting there, who gets jealous easily. You know what I'm talking about. Give that one your love and unconditional understanding.

- Now bring to mind, this one who is sitting there, who likes to overeat sometimes. Do you have that inside you? The part that binge eats and then feels bad about it... guilty and ashamed? Give that art your unconditional love and compassion.

- And finally, bring to mind, this one who is sitting there, who gets selfish and narcissistic.

The one who is desperate for attention and later regrets. Give that one the most love and compassion.

- Give your neurotic ego unconditional love, compassion and full understanding, that which you have been denying it all along.

- Now as you sit there, calm and centred, in the present moment, take all those parts of you that we went through and gave immense love to, integrate them all together. Own every single part of you… tie them all together like a bundle. That bundle is you.

- Realise that you exist. In this very moment it feels to you that you exist. Notice, that existence makes no judgements and assigns no value nor places any guilt or shame on your existence. The very fabric of existence accepts you exactly as you are. All that existence cares about is being / awareness. Not how you were or how you would be but exactly how you are right now, right here. Existence is never wrong. It either is or isn't but never both together. You are existence experiencing itself in absolute perfection. Notice that existence doesn't need you to be any other way than how you presently are. You might want to be any other way, but existence does not. We might say that existence gives you unconditional love because you simply are existing.

- Now give yourself that unconditional love and acceptance that existence gives you every moment of your life.

So, that is the process of self-acceptance. Keep doing this process over the next week at least (and whenever in the life, the situation calls for it). Just check in with yourself and remember that whatever is going on in your life and you are not satisfied with it... just stop there and be conscious enough of the fact that you need to give yourself more love and acceptance, rather than beating yourself up and acting out from a place of neurosis and resistance.

Whatever your sins or faults are, show them love and they will melt away. Give them pure acceptance. You don't have to slay these big dragons and hydra because every head you cut off a hydra a new one just comes up to replace it. This is what happens when you resist reality and it's a battle you can never win.

Don't expect overnight results with this as your shadow has solidified for years together. Do it over time (a few weeks to months) and I can assure you that the results are inevitable. You can always come back to this to ground yourself back into reality.

CHAPTER TEN

HOW TO STOP BEING JEALOUS

(With techniques)

Jealousy is a very tricky emotion. I'm a pretty emotionally self-aware person but jealousy still gets me. Not that it's often but that the thing that scares me about jealousy is that it is such a subtle emotion and it's so deceptive and hidden in the way that it acts. It can act on you for years and you won't even realise what's exactly going on. So, in this chapter we will proceed to speak upon the root causes of jealousy and how to cure it permanently with some really powerful ideas and solutions.

First, let's throw some specific examples here to ground this topic and not get too abstract. So of course, we have sexual jealousy and relationship jealousy to start off with. Another would be, getting jealous of the status that someone else has which could be anyone from your neighbour, boss, co-worker, competitor etc (who has something that you don't have). You could also be jealous about materialistic possessions and the attention that the person possessing it receives. Then of course, we have jealousy about beauty and external appearances.

The problem with jealousy is that a lot of times it masquerades as some other type of emotion. It might masquerade as anger, frustration, hatred, sadness, loneliness, criticism, trolling and basically a wide range negativity. Of course, when indulging in the above emotions we would rarely accept jealousy as the root cause or many a times be completely unaware of its presence. But here, we will turn the tables and use the sneaky nature of jealousy against itself to defeat it.

What really happens in the core of jealousy is that your identity feels threatened. By identity I mean the ego, self or simply 'me'. You have got a self-image in your mind about what you think you are and what you look like. You have got these self-beliefs and it's on level of these self-beliefs that we have to work. The fundamental thing here is that you have got a sense of self (self-image) that you want to protect. This self-image is illusory and has been covered in another chapter as it's too big to explain it here in a short burst. This sense of self is a concussion about all these ideas and beliefs you have about yourself and we believe that this stuff is very solid, real and tangible but actually it's not. Another lie is that you believe that this sense of self is very important for your success and well-being in life. Truth is this sense of self doesn't serve you in anyway, in fact it creates a lot of problems and suffering in your life, one of which and a major one is jealousy.

You are not happy and fulfilled on the inside because of this identity that you're trying to glorify and live up to all the time. So maybe you think of yourself as this very charming and wonderful person but in real life you don't get that feedback or maybe you believe that you are sexy and special but you feel threatened seeing your partner flirting with somebody else. This makes you extremely defensive and there are many different ways in which this defence mechanism can get triggered.

Also, be careful if you think that jealousy is only jealousy if it is externalized or getting broadcasted into the world by action or speech. Even triggered thoughts are manifestations of jealousy. The reason why you feel so bothered by the lack of feedback is because you think something really valuable is being taken away from you. This creates a distortion or imbalance internally as external reality contradicts your perceived self-image. The pain it causes makes you want to look away from the root cause.

The thing that you need understand is that the ego is all about looking away, it's all about self-deception. It never wants to acknowledge this giant ball of bulls**t that it is and this is why people are pretentious sometimes, trying to impress other people or trying to appear a certain way. They are not able to be themselves and authentic because they believe that if they were really authentic people wouldn't accept them and they wouldn't get enough emotional reciprocation from the external environment. So, they always have the burden of trying to live up to something extra.

When you feel a sense of external loss it's because you haven't found inner peace and you are not grounded internally. Therefore, any negative shift in the external environment can uproot your whole emotional balance and create havoc for you. You are relying on that external thing as a crutch (be it a person, wealth, status, attention etc). So, if that crutch is taken away you are afraid that you will fall flat on your face.

The only solution is to turn within. This is not a problem that gets solved externally although sometimes it may feel so but when the bandage peels off, jealousy will haunt you again. You are not going to win over jealousy by going out there and trying to one-up the person or situation. Don't get tricked by your ego into thinking that this is an external problem. You've to also convince yourself that jealousy is an ego game and it's not that you are actually threatened in anyway. Only then will you have the awareness and self-honesty to dive inner and look under the hood. Another thing to note here is that jealousy is extremely destructive and will prevent you from being the best version of yourself and creating an extra-ordinary life. You are not going to achieve great things if you are always on guard of somebody screwing you over somewhere.

Since you are reading this, it is evident that you want to be a good human being. A noble, self-actualized individual. Even if you don't know how to get there, the drive is the beginning just like the seed that will eventually grow into the oak tree. Right here, I want you to reflect on your life principles, your life values… what do you actually want out of life? Even if it's vague, that's alright, as long as there is something there because this is really important. Maybe there is this situation in your relationship or at work where you really wish you could get something a little bit more than you are currently getting. This is where your life principles come into play. Some examples would be honesty, justice, kindness, empathy, integrity, excellence, independence, creativity etc. I'm sure that nowhere in your top ten is there jealousy mentioned as a principle or value. In fact, you will find that jealousy is running against the very grain of what your top noble values are and that's very good. At least now you have grounded yourself outside of jealousy with a brighter vision.

Acknowledge to yourself right now that jealousy is a petty behaviour and it's below your standards. I also want you to picture right now whichever situation that you are jealous in, winning that situation using the jealousy strategy. So, the jealousy strategy usually goes something like this "well this person… I really hate this person because <insert criticism and judgement>" combined with initial passive aggressive behaviour. I want you to see the ramifications of that and picture how it's going to play out. So, you take this passive aggressive behaviour with some negative judgements in the mix or maybe you want to fight against them and take a more aggressive stance. Maybe you would subtly undermine what they are doing, sabotage their work or try to make them feel guilty in some sort of way. But now carry that through about what's going to happen as a result of that? What is the objective of this jealousy? You think it would improve your current state and make you feel better after you have acted out... it's supposed to give you more of something right?

Now, be honest to yourself... what will you acquire as the end result? And even if you do get something, will it make you genuinely happy? How are you going to feel about yourself using these tactics? What do you think that's going to do to you internally or psychological state? Will it be true victory? OR can you see that it's going to toxify everything. Even if you win using the jealousy strategy, you are going to actually lose because it's going to go against your life's principles and highest values. Carry that chain of thinking through and I want you to be very specific. I don't know what your situation is but I want you to actually visualise the chain of events that would follow and be very aware of how you are going to do it... and you will realise that ultimately it will not get you to where you want it to get you.

OR maybe you think that it might actually get you there. "maybe if I get my husband back or my girlfriend back, then that's going to be me getting what I want. So, what's wrong with that?". But see, you got to carry the psychological reasoning through. If that's what you are thinking then you have to understand that first of all you are trying to control a person here and controlling a person ever in life is already a huge red flag. Don't try to control people as that's a recipe for disaster. But let's say you do it anyway and you manipulate that person into coming back or being as you wanted. Now, you have to keep that control up constantly and this going to keep you in a constant fear state all time like a defensive bubble.

If you are jealous of someone's house and car and think if you get that you will be happy…no you won't. See, it's not about the house and car, it's about you. The jealousy may be supressed for a bit but will spring back up with another comparison soon. And this time, it will be stronger than before because you fed it by giving into it. No matter what the external objects are, if our internal mindset is not right, we will keep falling into infinite loops of jealousy time and again.

The way out of this is to notice. Just start to notice jealousy as it arises within you. Start to label it and you won't believe how much that right there will start turn the tide in your favour. Start to notice every single instance where you actually are jealous. Maybe you want to write them down. The technique used here is mindfulness which is observing the present moment without any judgement. Catch yourself being jealous in the moment and mentally label it. The trick here with mindfulness is that you don't want to judge yourself or make yourself feel guilty about it nor do you want to forcefully try to stop your jealousy prematurely. You want to be like a hunter watching its prey move through the forest. Just watch (with full alertness) the jealousy do it's nasty business in an objective and non-interfering manner. Although this is a simple process, it might be difficult for you because you are so unconscious while engaging in jealous behaviour. Keeping a jealousy log would be a great way to go about if this is really a major hurdle in your life. But just being fully aware of the jealousy as it's arsing and taking place, day after day, week after week, month after month, will autocorrect and dissolve it. Consistency is the key here.

Also notice, that this self-image you are trying to protect is just a bunch of thoughts and not as solid as you think it is. You can actually look through it and be like "you know what, why don't I take my self-image / ego and just set it aside for a moment and just be cool with the situation with resisting the current reality". Just start trying it out like that and see how you feel.

I also want you to be more appreciative of things. If you see your neighbour with that new car, do the exact opposite of what your ego wants to do in that moment. Instead of being defensive, open yourself up and appreciate the car like "oh that's a beautiful ride, good for him." Or if you see your partner speaking to a beautiful girl "oh that's a beautiful girl right there, she's got a great personality" rather than "oh that's a mean bitch who's going to ruin my relationship". Doing the exact opposite of what the ego is craving might seem a bit unnatural at first because you have been the ego's slave all your life, but eventually it will give you more freedom than you could ever fathom.

If you're a person with really low self-esteem then everything I'm saying here will seem a little too idealistic for you and I completely understand that but I encourage you to give this a serious try and see the results for yourself.

CHAPTER ELEVEN

WHAT IS WRONG WITH EGO

The ego is the cause of the majority of unhappiness you have in your life. It is the exact same mechanism of wrongness when you decide to spit into the wind. Quite obvious, the mechanism clearly backfires on you and the spit comes back at your face. Although the mechanism is same, for the ego it's a bit trickier than that because the ego likes to operate from self-deception. Before I get any further, I need to clarify what is ego.

Ego is nothing other than what you believe you are right now. It's not just some evil nefarious aspect of you or arrogance as commonly misperceived. It goes much deeper, in fact it's your whole identity. The very fact that you are sitting there right now and your entire life is revolving around you and your existence is ego. It is the entire identification that you have constructed. From your self-image to all the problems you think you have in your life, all the positive characteristics that you ascribe to yourself, all the beliefs that you hold, the personal story that you have inside your head, the very "I" of you. Most people take this for granted thinking that this is what life is and it's physically true but that is far from the truth. They are just ideas in your mind and images just vetted together in a rather arbitrary way but to you, because it is 'you', it seems unquestionable. This entire identity structure is the ego and the root cause of all your suffering in life.

Do not mistake the ego to be your existence. When you were born, you had no sense of identity. Your parents made you repeat and rote your identity, family name, school name, home address, national anthem and so on hundreds of times until they got drilled in your head and finally accepted those as your identity.

Following this all your experiences, emotions, expectations, mindsets and endeavours got deeply attached and integrated into this false sense of identity that you thought you were. As you grew up, the ego became stronger and bigger. Every day, every waking moment you spent in protecting the ego. The more you fed it, the more it rooted and solidified and you started seeing yourself on a higher illusory pedestal or let's say 'better self-esteem'. Even if you didn't, the ego made you chase it at all costs. The ego has cost you quite a bit and made life way tougher than what it really is. It did throw in a few good times but they were short and not entirely fulfilling in comparison to your expectations.

Majority of your actions up till now were an endeavour to enhance and protect the illusory identity that got drilled into you since childhood, for you mistook it for the real 'you'. Of course, the ego is required to function in society (as some individuality needs to be retained) but you cannot let the ego over power you. The ego should be your instrument and under your leash, not the other way around. Being aware of the ego and it's various manifestations will minimise your suffering to an extent you never imagined.

Until you start to become aware of how the ego creates most of your suffering, you would never really know what it feels like to be truly alive. What's really wrong about ego is every single problem you have in life and everything you hate about life. I want to show you how that it is but in order to show you we need to first get clear about what you hate about life.

Stop the reading here and right away make a quick list of the top 10 to 20 things that you don't like about your life, whatever they might be.

Let me present you a sample list right now (it's not mine) but just to get a common ground here:

- I hate having money problems.
- I hate my job.
- My spouse annoys me and my relationship is failing.
- My kids are getting bad grade in school.
- I feel depressed often and sometimes even have suicidal thoughts.

- I feel tired and bored with life.
- I don't have time for myself.
- My boss is an idiot.
- My parents are creating problems for me because they are so stubborn and dogmatic.
- The government is so corrupt.
- I'm scared of getting cancer.
- Losing weight is very difficult for me and I don't like how I look.
- In general, my life feels like an uphill battle all the time.

I'm hoping your list looks something like this too. Here's the shocker: what if I told you, all the stuff on your list is the result of ego and is not an inherent facet of life. Let that sink in for a moment. Majority would give a knee jerk reaction to this stating that this is how life is and there is not much that they can do about it. This in fact is their ego speaking in disguise in an attempt to run away from the problem, more so like a defence mechanism. It only appears that way because you've been living your life with a very strong ego and this list of problems is actually self-generated by the ego. It is a list of every backfiring or consequence of the ego. This might seem a bit far-fetched, for example you would ask how is the government being corrupt a problem of your ego? Or how are stubborn parents' consequence of one's ego? I'm saying yes, they are consequences of your ego. As I said earlier, the ego has very subtle and sneaky long-range consequences. It is not simply a matter of A causes B and B causes C, no. If you think about the consequences of ego in just these simple two or three chains of cause and effect, then what I'm implying won't seem plausible to you.

Instead, you would have to think about it more as A causes B, B causes C, C causes D, D causes E… all the way down the line to Z. This requires you to honestly examine the chain to see what's going on and I will help you to do that. For this, I would like to provide another list of typical problems that happen in the average person's life and it will be your job to investigate further how exactly is your ego responsible for these consequences. This is going to be a much bigger list than the previous one.

- Fear and anxiety. Every single fear and anxiety you've ever had in your life is created by the ego
- Anger, bitterness, hatred, violence and intolerance. All these are grounded in your ego and think about how much suffering it creates for you.
- Outrage and unfairness.
- Guilt and regret.
- Annoyances. Like the neighbour annoys you, the dog annoys you, spouse or kids? Believe it or not, that's very much tied with your ego.
- Criticism and blame. Pretty much all instances where you criticised or blamed is purely due to the ego and cannot exist without it.
- Depression

- Dissatisfaction.
- Shyness and insecurity.
- Acting out of integrity.
- Not liking yourself / physical appearance.
- Boredom, loneliness and neediness.
- Addictions. Could be drugs, porn, Tv, smartphone, binge eating… anything, it's all connected to your identity – the ego.
- Sexual misconduct or cheating.
- Lying, deception and manipulation.
- Self-sabotaging behaviours.
- Motivational problems.
- Indecisive.
- Feeling offended and self-righteous.
- Sadistic or masochistic.
- Dying a sorry death.

Do you realise that if you stay on the current track you're on, you'll die a very sorry death? Unless you are fortunate enough to die in an instantaneous fatal car crash or plane crash, chances are you going to die a slow death where you will have time to reflect on your life, actions and behaviours. What do you think you are going to feel on your death bed if you are dying a slow death? You'll realise on your death bed, how much of your life you've really wasted due to your ego.

By no means is that the end of the list as you can come up with more ways of how the ego creates suffering in life. Before we delve more into this, let me allow you to take you through the collective consequences of ego.

- Every single war in history can be traced back to ego.
- Genocide, conquering and extermination of other nations and peoples.
- Slavery.
- Scams, ponzi schemes and thefts.
- Abuse of children and women.
- Financial exploitation, capitalism and communism.
- Caste systems and power hierarchies.
- Corruption, bribery and nepotism.
- Religious intolerance.
- Cults and intellectual exploitations.
- Dictatorships, gangs and mafias.
- Political gridlock.
- Oppression of human rights and civil liberties.
- Pollution and destruction of nature. Well, this one is huge coming from the insatiable greed of mankind.

In the end we have got a very interconnected ecosystem that we are living in which includes the entire planet. As much as the ego likes to think that it's separate, it really isn't. the ego thinks that its separate, on a pedestal more special and important than everything else out there.

So, you probably ask what's the next step? Kill the whole identity i.e. kill yourself? Because all this sounds really anti-survival. Well, it is anti-survival but not to the extreme that you might think. The ego usually responds with a 'f**k you' to anything threatening its survival. What I'm telling you is to become more responsible for the way that you survive. Getting obsessed with survival and self-preservation is in fact way more detrimental than beneficial.

I also wish to clarify that I'm not claiming the go to be absolutely bad and inherently evil. It's bad in a sense that obsession with it creates suffering for you. I'm not demonising the ego but instead trying to make you aware of how it backfires.

A simple formula: Happiness = 1/ego (They are inversely proportionate to each other)

If you realise this, you hit the core of all personal development which is basically being aware of the go. Becoming so aware of it that it starts to chip off and dissolve.

Don't mistake the lessening of ego i.e. less of "I" would indicate less happiness. In fact, you experience true raw bliss which has no substitute.

As an assignment for the next week (or next month, however long you want it to be) is to notice on a very moment to moment daily level when you are suffering and then to connect that to the ego. As yourself, "how is my identity producing this suffering that I'm experiencing right now?". It's an extremely powerful question and it's not easy to ask that when you're in the midst of suffering because at that time all you care about is removing the suffering with a quick temporary solution. You don't care about looking at the suffering very carefully and tracking it to its root cause and that's why it repeatedly haunts you again and again.

CHAPTER TWELVE

WHAT SHOULD YOU BE AFRAID OF? (HARSH MOTIVATION)

What is the one thing that is worth fearing in your life? What is the one thing that you should fear tonight... and every night for the rest of your life? Take a guess. On our self-development journey we try to eliminate fears through emotional self-mastery but what's perhaps one fear that is trespasses the bounds of personal growth yet is a healthy fear to have? to remind you every once in a while, so you don't backslide or get complacent.

The biggest thing you should fear in your life, is that you waste your life. This precious thing that you've got, this one chance, this one instance, this one shot... just one, you only get one. I don't consider myself special or extra ordinary than others, but one place where I do stand out is that I recognise deeply that I've got just one life and it's passing by every single moment. That means something special to me and that I've to make something special out of it. Everything in my life gets reverse engineered around this one realisation.

Every time my friend and I used to go to the club, we used to joke that we are living our lives right now, every day, as though we are having a mid-life existential crisis. Then we would go on to look and point out people who would seem to have mid-life crisis 10 to 20 years from now. But we were happy that the existential crisis had come upon so early because in the end, during death, you are only going to have regrets over the things you did not do. In my life, I feel I've already gone through two existential crises and I'm not even 25 yet. I think that's healthy because I see people stumbling through life, unmotivated, petty, shallow, pursuing things that they don't know why they are pursuing them, busy: running around like hamsters on a wheel... and I've been guilty of this till some extent but somewhere in the back of my mind in the large scale, I've never really lost track of what the ultimate objective is. That is to make something special of your life. To make sure that every single month and year of your life, you're staying on track with something big and special.

Is that what you want? To lead a basic life with a 9 to 5 job and then retirement. Is that what you are going to do with your one life? That's it? You're going to go, punch the clock for 8 to 9 hours a day, for 40 years of your life doing work that you have no emotional connection to, doing work that isn't serving the world in any especially important way, come home and sit in front of the TV… and you're going to do this over and over and over again. Maybe once you retire, you'll go fishing somewhere or just travel once in a while… really? Is that what your life is going to be? Is that what you are going to do with this one life?

Do you realise what this life is? I feel people don't really understand what this life is. I mean, look at your hands right now, look around you… it's pure magic.

12 or 14 billion years ago, there was supposedly a big bang. Before that there was who knows what? Not even nothingness. From that big bang came out all the matter and energy taking billions of years for all that to cool down and create stars. Those stars morphed and drew in dust clouds, created planets, exploded again and again, creating heavier elements until more and more denser planets could be formed. 4 billion years ago, we got the Earth. The Earth was just a molten ball of lava, it then cooled until finally little organisms started to run around it. Then we had 3 and a half billion years of evolution. This amazing thing… if you ever studied the complexity and richness of evolution, it blows your mind and brings you to tears learning how intricate everything is and how well it all works together. From that arose reptiles, amphibians and dinosaurs followed by an apocalypse around 65 million years ago that wiped out the dinosaurs and nearly everything from the face of the earth. This allowed the mammals to rise following 10 to 15

million years of evolution until primates started to become more like what humans are now. From that there was a whole series of progression up to the homo sapiens and that's what you are.

From there we had more hundreds and thousand years of evolution of civilisation, language, culture, technology and art etc. Finally, here we are in the 21st century now… and what about you? When your mom and dad got together, the average woman has around 150 to 200 eggs in her whole life and the average man secretes around 150 million sperm per act… think about what are the odds of you being materialised from that? Well, you beat those odds. Not only that, you were also gestating for 9 months in your mom's stomach going through 9 months of pregnancy successfully. Many pregnancies don't go through successfully. So, you made it through that and you were born relatively healthy, un-deformed, with your limbs and eyesight intact. Do you realise what you are? You're not a one thing. You're an amalgamation or giant country as it were of 40 trillion individual living cells (that's what scientists estimate). We are now in the 21st century with so many advancements, you live in a good country with relatively good political and military stability, decent economy, no slavery anymore, no serious wars happening, good laws, amazing technology, the internet… basically right now is the freest and most amazing time to have been a human being ever, in the history of the universe. That's where you're living right now.

Beyond that, what is this reality? It's like pure magic. Yet what have you done with this magical thing? You've made yourself bored, miserable, depressed, whining and complaining, acting the victim, being unmotivated, worrying about stupid things, holding negative judgements or opinions about other people and things, taking everything for granted when in fact you should be on your knees thanking whatever gods you believe in, that this stuff exists.

The worst thing you do is keeping yourself busy with stupid sh*t. So busy... "oh but my life, my life is so full, my life is so important, I've got kids, job, bills to pay, so many obligations" ... Bullsh*t. Those are petty stupid little things and the busier you are, the pettier your life is.

I challenge you to live a noble life. Take whatever goals you have for your life (your highest aspirations and visions) and multiply that into 10. Not because I'm telling or not because you want to leave a legacy behind... none of that matters, everyone's going to forget about you in a couple of generations no matter how successful you are. But you yourself will care when you're lying on your death bed about what you did with your life and how all those petty 'busy' moments robbed you of your precious existence on this planet.

What if I told you that you only had till the end of today to live. Soak that in and just imagine that it was the case right now. How would you feel? Suddenly how precious would everything become? Would you still be 'busy' with all that 'important stuff'?

Make your goals and aspirations less about you and more about the beauty of life. What's your work doing to advance the universe that you're living in? Are you proud of the work you're doing? If life gave you a second chance all over again, would you choose the same work and life course? If not, set some noble goals right now. As I said above, multiply your goals by 10. If you decide you want to go teach 50 people, instead go teach 500 people. If you decide that you want to create a green energy company, go make it 5 to 10 times bigger than you planned. Or go help the environment, society or the world in a 10 times more powerful, beautiful and noble way.

See how that makes you feel, when you begin to think along those lines because you know what? You've got a very tiny bit of time left which will pass by before the universe takes another breathe.

CHAPTER THIRTEEN

HOW TO STOP CARING WHAT PEOPLE THINK OF YOU

Why do we allow other people to have so much control over the way we live our lives? If you are a people pleaser / attention seeker and you find this topic resonates with you and you want to stop caring so what everyone's thinking about you then I'm going to help you to take a deep look behind this. Although all of us face it, some people face it to such a large degree that it's crippling their lives not to mention the root of social anxiety. This also happens to be a personal topic for me because this is something that I really had to struggle with for a long time. Over the last couple of years, I've made some really big and penetrative progress regarding this. I have some mindsets that I want to share with you so right at the end of this chapter you can walk away with some big paradigm shifts.

When you're walking down a street, do you think 'how do I look in his/her eyes?'. When you're on the phone with someone, do you think 'oh, how are they going to interpret that?'. If you're talking to a group of colleagues at work, in the back of your mind you're always running that analysis of how you will come off. Do you regularly go out of your way to supress conflict or maintain your image in other's eyes?

Let's take a look at why this is happening here. You've got an image of yourself in your mind, you've got this mental picture of what you think you're like. We all have this but you as a people pleaser / attention seeker have an inflated self-image that is kept alive due to massive doses of external validation. Not to mention the bloated moral high ground and strong need to be perceived as a good and kind hearted human being that you imagine yourself to be, your ideal self. It's not enough that you have this image but you also desperately seek to have this image reflected in the external circumstances. You want external evidence that your image is perfect and accurate. You want this evidence from your boss, your parents, siblings, spouse, friend circle, clients or in fact even random strangers. You want all of them to validate your inflated and illusory self-image. You want to approved off and because of this, you are working very hard to maintain this image. As you can already guess, when you got all these people in your life that you are trying to please and want certain emotional reactions from, that's not such an easy thing to get. It's not an easy situation to architect.

The problem gets so deep that you try to architect your whole life around pleasing others / seeking attention to gain maximum approval and acceptance which in turn upholds your self-image of 'I'm such a good human being <insert any other approval>'. Why? Because, 'he said so, she said so, they said so, they wrote about me here, it was told about me there'. You are hunting for that conformation evidence time and again. Anytime you hear evidence that is contradicting the self-image, it really disturbs you.

While being empathetic can be very nice but for you it's a trap. Here's a fundamental problem that you need to come to in grips with: although it's nice to care about other people and care about their opinions, you're a living and breathing organism. This organism that consists of 40 trillion cells, each one of them fighting for its own individual survival. You don't even realise how incredibly self of an organism you are at a meta level. To deny this nature within you is a challenge because you're rubbing against the very core of your humanity, which is survival at all costs. When you put the feelings and priorities of everybody else over your own at all times, then you're putting yourself in this adversarial relationship with your own nature because your own nature is going to fight back. Maybe it would take it for some time but not indefinitely, therefore problems start to arise. You cannot supress this stuff leading to build up of anger, resentment, feeling of low self-esteem / self-worth, unfulfilled, feeling inauthentic, lack of reciprocal gratitude in your various relationships. In the end, it is preventing you from building your dream life.

Don't misinterpret this as me telling you to turn into a selfish a-hole. The thing is you do not let your brain bully you by engaging in black and white thinking or only looking at extremes. Of course, if you're reading this book, you've no intention of becoming an a-hole and believe being on the 'goodie goodie' side although has certain pitfalls, is the higher road to take. It doesn't have to be this way. I'm going to give you a new alternative which is to take the middle way.

A person on the middle path does take into consideration external feedback but is also grounded strongly on internal values and self-love. This is the path that you have to eventually embody if you want to create an extra ordinary life. Also, the middle path is a very sustainable strategy for long terms whereas the other two are kind of 'crash and burn' and short sighted.

So what is an opinion? That which somebody is thinking about you? It's basically a thought in somebody else's head. Think over this: you're letting a figment of somebody else's imagination literally control your life. When put like this, it sounds ludicrous that you would do this and yet you slip into that same ditch time and again. It's okay to pay heed to the figments of imagination in the minds of your close ones and that's healthy until you start giving into the figments of imagination of complete strangers. This is nothing other than lack of complete internal grounding which could be based on either emotional or logical internal consistencies.

An example: you don't even know half the people in the audience and yet you care about how they perceive you and you want to create a flawless image of yourself in their head. It's really a pity to see a person in such a state of lose internal grounding.

You're on your date and you're so worried that this person whom you've known for a couple of hours/days is judging you, what are they thinking about you or what is going on in their mind. You are letting this dictate how your life progresses... do you realise how ridiculous that is? It may pass off as normal without any level of introspection but one deep look will show you the amount of emotional insecurities beneath it. This is really a travesty because you are taking all the power and responsibility you have to direct your life and giving it away to external sources. No one should have that kind of power over you but your own self.

You see, praise and criticism both are really just two sides of the same coin. The higher you are need for praise and acceptance, the more sensitive you're to criticism. You cannot separate the two.

One objection that might come up here – feedback. Don't I need feedback? If I'm making this art, doing something in a relationship, selling a product etc then isn't feedback needed? Well… the problem here is your weak internal guiding system that uses external opinions as sheer benchmarks or goal posts rather than arbitrary pointers. So, a person with strong internal values can listen to feedback and take in external opinions but they won't get irrational or neurotic about it.

Most people pleasers / attention seekers don't look for genuine feedback. What they do look for is validation and approval because preservation of that self-image supersedes authentic feedback and criticism for them. It's like ego mania masquerading as feedback. Be careful about your ego telling you that you're selfless because that's the time when you're probably being the most selfish by continuously feeding the ego's self-image.

You might also object by saying that if you didn't receive proper feedback, it might throw you off course, arguing that the people in your life help you to constantly stay on track. Yes, sometimes it's good to have people to hold you accountable and do sanity checks but you don't want that to become a crutch / way of life.

We all are aware about the backlashes of being sensitive to criticism but what about praise? What's wrong in a nice compliment here or there? Technically there is nothing wrong with praise but the problem is when you get neurotic about it. You crave it to prop up this ideal self-image that you've got (which is in reality, a total fiction). When you don't get the praise that you think you deserve (which happens so often) you begin to doubt yourself, lose self-esteem and get bitter.

You need to come to the realisation right now and admit to yourself that the strategy you're using of constantly seeking approval is crap and it's time to drop it. Most people pleasers won't even get this far. They don't like being people pleasers at their core but they seldom take this first step of thinking it all through, 'wait a minute… this is a strategy I'm using. An overarching life strategy and it cannot be sustained anymore'. This might induce fear in you as it will expose / challenge you to step into a completely different paradigm, away from your comfort zone along. Your brain will come up with the most seemingly rational explanations to try to keep you grounded in your current strategy but you need to bust through that and realise that for you the best strategy is to become independent. Independent of other's opinions. So, when people do praise you, you will humbly accept it but you won't need that praise and it won't change your trajectory. Also, if people constantly criticise you, laugh at you or doubt your worth, it's okay because you won't get triggered by it.

This game that you're playing (upholding your self-image at all costs) cannot be won because you're trying to make every opinion out there, exactly the way you want. Basically, you're trying to control the imaginations of other people – it's nuts and will never play out as per your fantasies. Also, opinions are very random and capricious in nature.

A lot of times what people think about you says very little about you and instead more about them. Think about the time when you were in a bad mood… maybe you'd got a flat tire earlier that morning on your way to work or you skipped breakfast / coffee and now you're cranky or you had an argument with your spouse and in that state, somebody else comes to you asking for your feedback on something or you're having a conversation which you chime into, what happens? You'll be negative and so will your opinions and perceptions.

Look how random and groundless opinions and judgements are. Do you want surrender your dreams and aspirations to the randomness of the external world?

Ask yourself this: Can you lead an extra ordinary life if you're dependent on random circumstances?

It's okay for the following things to happen:

- It's Okay for someone to think you're an a-hole.
- It's Okay for someone to think that your work is sh*t.

- It's Okay if someone mocks you, ridicules you or makes fun of you.
- It's Okay if you don't get that compliment which you think you deserve to get.

You need to learn to treat these things as the wind blowing. The wind would be blowing left one morning and right the next morning. The truth is no human being or external source can fulfil you, if you aren't internally grounded. Reversely, no human being or external source can dissatisfy you, if you are truly grounded from within. Accept the fact that your self-image will get tarnished and people out there won't be constantly validating it.

A few more okay's:

- It's Okay to challenge / confront people.
- It's Okay to offend people once a while.
- It's Okay to hold an unpopular opinion.
- It's Okay to not fit in all the time.
- It's Okay to not be the average of society's expectations.
- It's Okay for people to criticise or dislike you for being your authentic self.
- It's Okay for people to think your opinions are invalid.

A people pleaser's initial reaction would be extremely averse to these but the more they go out and start putting these into practice, they will realise that it was never that serious and doesn't really matter as much as they thought. This would help build a tougher skin and some tolerance.

I rather have a clash with an authentic person because even the clash would be on authentic grounds rather than gel in with a people pleaser who puts on a mask to get by. I mean, how fake does it feel? No one wants the empathy of an inauthentic and unhealthy individual.

Assignment:

For the next 90 days (assuming you have severe people pleasing tendencies), for 5 minutes, you are going to repeat this affirmative statement with full focus – 'I am completely independent of the good or the bad opinion of others'.

The above affirmation is really powerful to reprogram your subconscious mind. You would be surprised at the end of 90 days that how something as simple as this can bring in a radical shift in perception. Don't dismiss this by falsely believing that it will make you cold-hearted and unempathetic. Instead it will empower you with more compassion minus the ego's selfish needs or fears.

CHAPTER FOURTEEN

HOW TO BE STRATEGIC (Quick-short guide)

For the following topic, I won't go into details as to each their own but I will provide precise key pointers that will help you to be more strategic in literally anything. This can be applied to short/long term and all kinds of goals and can be highly personalised.

Strategic thinking is setting goals and developing flexible long-range plans to reach those goals based on careful analysis of internal and external environments.

Most common strategic blunders:

- Lack of critical thinking
- Wasting the prime years of your life
- Eating junk food
- Addiction to various things and social media
- Not developing mastery in any field
- Not working towards self-actualization
- Not continuing education after college
- Staying loyal to dysfunctional/negative people
- Investing money in wrong places
- Going into debts / using excessive credit cards

- Being too cheap to hire life coach and self-help material
- Living in the wrong place with the wrong people
- Chasing sex / devoting lots of time to it
- Neglecting meditation / yoga / any other activity for mind-body union

Failures of strategy:
- Not doing the right thing at the right time. (not being able to think macro / big picture)
- Unable to delay gratification. (there cannot be a strategy if you are chasing immediate gains)
- Lacking intel / research
- Lacking knowledge of oneself (strengths / weaknesses)
- Always reacting, not acting.
- Chasing the small prize, rather than the larger prize.
- Most people just do what lands on their lap, without questioning / critical analysis.
- Oblivious to social / business traps
- Not investing time into strategizing
- Not fixing problems at their root.

I   Strategic intent

- It is a compelling vision of the future that
  motivates action.
- Have a very clear vision of the future.
- Backwards engineering every step needed to
  get there.
- Everything that you do has to be methodically
  aligned towards the strategic intent.

II   Strategic analysis

- SWOT analysis of the whole situation. (swot –
  strength / weakness / opportunity / threat)
- Do you have the resources available to go
  ahead? If no, how do you acquire them and
  arrange them methodically to gain maximum
  leverage?
- These include mental energy, time, willpower,
  interactions etc
- Anticipate various potential / future scenarios.
- It's not static, its flexible and yet bound to the
  original intent.

III   Strategic preparation

- Building up of strategic reserves through
  preparation.
- Hard work / discipline

- Thorough training
- Sharpening strengths
- Working on weaknesses
  [since you cannot predict what the future will hand you, you must develop yourself internally to handle external circumstances]

IV Concentration of force

- This decisive point is the key to all strategy. It is all about directing your full force and determination given your limited resources.

V Detailed execution

- A great plan poorly executed leads to disaster.

VI Adaptability

- Understand that the environment is constantly changing every day.
- Plan for emergencies / mishaps.
- Keep aligning your goal to reality and remain open minded.

VII Study of general principles

- Regardless of how chaotic a situation maybe there are always principles to guide you and help you navigate, think clearly and give deeper insights.
- Not just looking for a fix.
- Seeking a deep understanding / mastery.

CHAPTER FIFTEEN

HOW TO FORGIVE SOMEONE

First let us make a distinction between true forgiveness and half-hearted forgiveness, something which a lot of people don't understand. Most people don't do true forgiveness and the difference between the two is very stark. While some may even forgive in the moment, they find it difficult to make it stick.

Let's crack into the different situations in which you might want to forgive someone (but is tough to):

- Cheating and lying
- Abuse (emotional or physical)
- Fits of anger and violence
- Being treated unfairly

Just wrong behaviour in general of any sought. In all these situations you need to develop a strong ability to forgive because if you do not know how to forgive people then that means your relationships are fragile. If you really want to maintain a relationship with someone for a long period of time then you need to hone your forgiving skills because invariably mistakes will creep up and you need something to weather those mistakes.

See, most people make a mistake of thinking that it comprises of only one component that is 'let go'. So, they let go but don't forget therefore repeatedly pondering and ruminating on what hurt them which in turn keeps it alive. It's kind of like a scab i.e. a wound that's healing but you keep picking at it all the time, making the situation worse. This is exactly what happens when you do half-hearted forgiveness.

During true forgiveness, you're creating a completely new slate and you are not reliving those moments from the past. The past only stays with you till the extent that you're reliving it again and again.

Another trap with the half-hearted forgiveness is that is also becomes a self-righteous forgiveness. That means you feel proud of yourself for forgiving the other person and feeling noble which is no different than keeping score. This puts your ego on the pedestal and gives you an air of superiority so next time if there is any conflict the ego would love to pull out the score card and subtly throw the other person into submission. This rather than healing a situation induces more toxicity than before. You've only forgiven them superficially as your actions are passive aggressive and the layer of resentment is still lingering. That's not the point of forgiveness.

You've to completely forget the wrong done and that's a conscious decision that you've to make. Also, I'm not asking you to become a doormat by forgiving everyone for everything they did. If someone cheats on you in nice long relationship, you don't have to forgive them and then tolerate it. If your boundaries have really been crossed and every internal value violated then don't forgive that person if you wish not to. You can reinforce your boundary and break the relationship off do whatever you got to do. But if you think that it is repairable or there is something still valuable here that can be salvaged and the opposite party is honestly regretful about their actions then you can make the conscious choice of forgiving that person.

When you make the conscious choice of forgiveness, it's not a pact between you and them but rather a pact between you and you. You are making a promise to yourself to let it go, right now and to never think about it again. The other person has a very small role to play in forgiveness (no matter how counter intuitive that sounds) because to truly forgive a person it takes a lot of inner strength and courage. Yes, the 'forgetting' part is tough as the mind will keep thinking and visualising about the negative things done to you. So, you have to summon courage and fortitude to stay on track with your original promise. If anytime it comes into your mind randomly, you take the conscious decision of not engaging in it.

If you're not willing to do that and you give into every instant of it flashing in your brain then toxicity is going to build up and you're going to create this revengeful type of forgiveness. That might be able to hold things together for a short while but eventually it will explode. You have the option of letting go of it right now but the real question is, do you want to?

"True forgiveness is when you realise that you've no reason to hate or judge the other person in the first place." – Maxwell Maltz (Psycho-cybernetics)

You might think that you do have reason to hate / judge but to live this quote you've to summon your inner nobility and courage.

Honestly, one of the main reasons why you're having issues with forgiveness is because you don't have a strong enough direction in your life. See, our minds love being engaged and if you don't feed it enough with your direction / life purpose, it will default into ruminating and knit picking the more pettier issues and the past. So, is your mind working to create or is it just sitting ideally and going through old data gravitating you towards a negative loop.

Go ahead and make the conscious decision right now.

CHAPTER SIXTEEN

HOW TO LET GO OF THE PAST

Every one of us has something in the past that:

- Haunts us
- Hinders our performance
- Something we keep going back to
- Traumatic
- Induced fear
- Made us retreat into our shell
- Robbing us of our energy
- Anxious about it occurring again and always on guard

The first point I want to make is that it is very possible to let go of the past no matter how bad your past is. I'm referring to very serious traumas like rape, death of a loved one, divorce, loss of a child, bankruptcy, childhood abuse, near death experiences... you can let it all go, I promise you. The question is, are you willing to put in the effort and work towards letting it go?

You should really let it go because a negative experience from the past is not doing anything positive for you in the moment. One of the main reasons you're holding on to it is because you think that if you do let it go then somehow your life will worsen and you'll open yourself up to threats again. I can relate to this feeling as I've been there and I still do have some hang-ups. But these hang-ups sometimes rob me of my current performance although I've worked through majority of them.

You need to understand what the past is. You think the past is so real, so vivid, feels just like yesterday but the past is not real. It's just a concept which was real at some point of time but it does not exist anymore. The future by the way is not real as well and is also a concept. The only thing real is the 'now', right now, this very moment. That's reality and everything else is a thought inside your head which called conceptualisation. You're investing a lot of emotional charge and attributing a lot of reality into something that actually isn't real.

That problem you think is going to happen tomorrow at work is not real but rather just a concept. You might counter this by saying you're very sure how something negative would pan out tomorrow... no you don't and that's still just a concept. The whole world could end tomorrow in a meteorite apocalypse for all we know. That doesn't mean that you should dismiss critical thinking and strategy but you need to understand that the future and especially the past are mere concepts and do not exist at any given point of time. The past cannot be pointed towards nor revisited / relived. The past is just a memory in your head and I agree that sometimes those memories can get lodged really deep rooting itself firmly in your mind.

As an exercise now, I want you to think of something that is still traumatic from your past and you want to let go, right now: (spend a while on each point)

- Bring that back up and feel the negativity it is causing.
- Let it be there and don't try to resist it.
- Now sit back and relax as I guide you further along.
- I want you to notice your breathe and feel it going in / coming out.
- Breathe in / out nice and slow and keep all your awareness on it.

- Now I want you to put all your attention into your body. Feel all the sensations in your body from feet, through your legs, thighs and your butt sitting on the cushion, through your back, up into your shoulders, all the way to your face, head, arms and fingertips. Relax all your muscles especially your facial and shoulder muscles.

- Now let's play an imagination exercise. I want you to pretend that you have no future. The future is non-existent and you're totally in the present right now.

- I want you to imagine that the past never happened, there was no past at all, you just are right now and you always were… in the right now in the moment. Your perceptions and sensations that you're having right now is your body and as you listen to me is reality and nothing else exists. Don't think about it, just soak it in and be in the moment.

- Take a few last deep breathes with full awareness of the present moment and end the exercise.

You can always go back and do the exercise. If you honestly did this, you got into the moment or what is real. Do you understand now that the rest is just concept?

You might argue saying that the past may not be real but it still affects you or the future is not real but the 'now' will turn into the future at some point and it will become real. True, I agree but this one exercise for a few minutes won't detach you from the past instantly. You'll have to keep coming back to the exercise every time the past comes to haunt and slowly you will build resistance to it to a point where your awareness will not drift into the concept of past even if you force it to… and that's an amazing state to achieve.

One of the limiting beliefs that you're holding is you thinking that you cannot let go of the past which is completely false. If that belief is shattered, you are already half way through. Well, you just got rid of it for two minutes or however long that exercise lasted for you. This is such a strong realisation to have that the past only exists because you keep bringing it back up.

Don't over complicate it or make it tougher than it really is. Do you think worrying or brooding over it will somehow prevent that mistake or event from reoccurring? No, it won't but it will probably lead to some sort of self-fulfilling prophecy effect.

CHAPTER SEVENTEEN

FAKE GROWTH VS REAL GROWTH

(What if you're just tricking yourself)

It's very easy to deceive yourself when you're ding personal development into thinking that you're actually growing when really, you're not fixing the root issues that are causing the deepest problems in your life. In general, what I find is when we enter personal development, those first few years we spend in orienting ourselves unsure of how the whole thing would integrate in our lives. We have these cartoon caricatures in our heads of what growth will look like.

People get into personal development because they want a solution to a burning problem in their lives and in their minds, they imagine in almost a childlike way of what the solution is going to look like or how the issue is going to be resolved for them. It's funny because some of these expectations and caricatures are so unreal that it points them in the wrong direction as to where to look for solutions.

Let's say we got a shy guy with low confidence who comes saying. 'I want to become really confident and my solution to this problem is to become the super alpha confident guy.' Then he goes looking for that thinking that's really going to resolve the issue by becoming a super alpha confident guy. Of course, that's not how it will get resolved.

Or a woman comes into personal development looking for prince charming, 'I'm getting needy, lonely and my life is kind of empty. If I could just find prince charming, then that's going to bring me happiness.' Again of course, that's not how it will work.

No deep issue gets resolved with your fantasy solutions. In reality, when you experience real growth, the issue simply becomes a non-issue. So, if you're shy with crippling social anxiety, the solution is not to become this super alpha male but rather to stop caring about the shyness. You don't counter internal problems with external solutions… that's not personal development. So, you may probably still remain the same beta male that you are but shyness and social anxiety will no longer fall in your way because you've penetrated your psych deep enough to uproot those issues form their source. If you're feeling needy, the solution is not to get a partner to fill in the void (which is nothing other than feeding the issue more) but to actually stop feeling needy. There's an emotional release after which you stop caring about the issue altogether. There is a huge shift in perspective and that's what real growth looks like compared to fake growth.

So, how do you know that you've experienced real growth in any area of your life? You get a permanent release of the issue. You don't over compensate for it and you stop obsessing over it. Also, you won't need any defensiveness anymore. A lot of people think that in order to resolve their issue they need to build a giant fortress around it, with electrical barb wiring and mortars to protect it from attacks. You can build all the security systems you want but the problem is still there and it will still haunt you in the back of your mind. No matter what you do, that castle will fall in future and the more secured you tried to make it the more it will hurt you. The only solution is to bring it down on your own and erase it completely so there is nothing left in there to protect. That's true freedom.

Dismantling all your defences sounds very counter intuitive and scary to the ego because the ego only understands defensiveness and protectiveness.

Another hallmark of true growth is that there is no longer any need to exert willpower over the situation. There is no longer a need to whip yourself into a frenzy. Also gauge your emotional reaction to those particular triggers and see how / when your buttons get pushed.

Fake growth masquerades as real growth and a lot of effort is misdirected towards creating temporary external fixes. These fixes aim at fixing external circumstances not realising that the root of the issue lies within. In a very clever way they take the attention of the real issue which is inside and unfortunately remains unattended. Real growth is not getting what you're chasing for externally but releasing the desire to chase it internally.

CHAPTER EIGHTEEN

DROPPING THE ROLES, YOU PLAY

"You wore a mask for so long that you forgot who you were beneath it" – Anonymous.

Have you noticed yet how majority of us tend to live our lives acting out roles? These roles are obvious to everyone around them but opaque to themselves and probably you fall under this too. You're not aware that you are playing a role which is actually a contrivance. So, I want to help you see that in yourself and possibly move towards dropping some of it.

I will present a list of roles to give a clear idea but in the abstract what I mean by a role is like a costume that you put on or character that you are which you picked up throughout your life. You've been wearing the costume for so long that you've confused it for your authentic personality.

Imagine an alien looking down on earth from outer space. He looks at the entire narrative of your life and he can clearly spot the role that you are / were playing. What will that be for you? Can you start to suspect what your own contrivances might be? Sometimes how silly they are and yet how seriously you take them? These roles could be personal, career and business, family life and so forth.

So, here's the list and look closely for a couple of roles that have really stuck to you for a good chunk of your life:

- The perfectionist
- The rebel
- The alpha male
- Mr. Cool
- The bad ass
- The winner
- The loser
- The player
- The nice guy
- The victim
- The smart ass
- The responsible one
- The mysterious one
- The socialite
- The attention seeker
- The martyr
- The geek
- The guru
- The con artist
- The soccer mom
- The professional

This list shows only a tiny portion of all the possible roles. The question I have for you is who were you before you picked up roles? And you did pick them up, no one is born with them. Go back to the time before you had picked up a particular role and try to remember how different life was. Let some of those early memories come back to you. What was it like when you were living without most of the obligatory roles?

What vulnerability did you want to mask or where did you want to fit in when you first started to pick up a particular role? At first when you put on the costume it probably didn't feel authentic but then over time as you started getting more and more used to it, it started feeling like a second skin to you.

One of the key themes of personal development is shedding the false layers and unmasking your most authentic self. To begin to unmask a role you've just start getting aware of and begin to see how artificial and contrived it is. Like an ape putting on a tuxedo and walking around like he's James Bond. When it becomes quite transparent to you and you realise the absurdity of it, then it will naturally dissolve on its own.

Worksheet (Try to be honest, accurate and concrete):

-   What are the top 3 roles you play?

- What are the most common and specific ways in which you act out those roles?

- How did you acquire each role? What event (trauma, sudden need to adapt etc) created the need for those roles?

- How are those roles protecting you? What vulnerability / insecurity are they masking?

- Which deep psychological needs does playing each role satisfy?

- How would your life be without these roles?

- Do you desire full authenticity with absolutely no compromise?

- How could you be more self-aware while playing inside of a role?

CHAPTER NINETEEN

VALUE ASSESSMENT

(A complete guide on finding your core values and making them your ultimate reality)

I   *Value assessment Intro:*

"The story of the human race is the story of men and women selling themselves short." – Abraham Maslow

Why are values so important?

- Values determine happiness and are the blue print for happiness in your own life.
- They define your authentic self.
- They make tough decisions easy to make.
- Define the domain where your life purpose is.
- Makes goal setting and prioritization easy.

Your values are like a list of priorities – the things you find most meaningful in your life. you can feed any decision into your values to see which the ideal one is. One of the secrets of life is to stop doing stuff that doesn't make you happy – sounds simple right? Then why haven't you implemented it completely?

Clarifications and warnings:

- We are talking about the things you actually value and not the things that you wish you valued. Your true values are often masked by social and cultural pressure. Society creates trap values that aren't authentically yours.
- Positive values – what you move towards.
- Negative values – what you move away from. You have quite a few of negative values (negative motivations) but still put them down.
- You've to be very self-honest in this process.

II *Most meaningful things in your life:*

"Mental energy is not a fixed substance. It rises and falls with our passion and commitment to what we are doing at that time." – Ken Robinson

Exercise:

- Sit down in a quiet place with a pen and a notepad for 20 minutes (or however long this may take you, don't try to rush).
- On top of the notepad write – what is *most meaningful* to me in my life.
- Brainstorm – start jotting down various answers.
- Ask the question over and over again – what is *most meaningful* to me in my life?
- If it feels right, write it down.

143

- Use emotion and intuition.
- Try to get at least 15 different items.
- Attempt to boil similar items down to an essence.
- Use clear and precise language.

III *Tabula rasa:*

"Do not be misled by a false notion of obligation or duty. You can owe no possible obligation or duty to others which should prevent you from making the most of yourself. Be true to yourself and you cannot be false to any other man." – Wallace Wattles

Exercise:

- Sit down with a pen and paper for 15 minutes.
- Close your eyes and imagine before jotting down the answers.
- Imagine if you could live your life all over again from the scratch while keeping your current experiences and wisdom.
- Also imagine that you've no major obstacles in your way.
- Imagine you have got 70 years to live and you want this thing to be a work of beauty. Something you can look back at on your death bed and say 'yup, that was really a well-lived life.'

- Ask yourself – what 10 things should your life be about?
- What this life is focussed on are the pillars on which this life stands.
- Write short, concise, specific and tangible ideas.
- Don't be vague by giving pillars like 'peace', 'happiness'. You must have concrete tangible answers for 'what does this mean for me?'

IV *Master values list:*

"Individuals who depart from the norms like heroes, saints, sages, artists and poets as well as madmen and criminals, look for different things in life than most others do" – M. Csikszentmihalyi

It's likely that you must have forgotten some values of yours during the first two exercise.

Exercise:

- Scout the list made above.
- Contemplate over each value with the intention of finding your top 10.
- Compare the results of your first two exercises with the top ten values that you chose here.
- These would be the top ten values you would abide by if you were to create an amazing life from the scratch.

- The most important thing is here being what these values mean to you and not anyone else.

V   *Toxic values:*

Exercise:

- Now look at your top ten list and identify what you feel are toxic values.
- Reconsider replacing those (quite obvious).
- Happiness / fulfilment shouldn't be on the list because that's the final objective.
- Move the toxic values to a new list.
- Plug the holes in top ten list again.

VI   *Value definitions:*

"You want to live, but tell me, is the life you are living currently any different form the dead?" – Seneca

Don't take that quote too literally but I'm sure you got its underlying message. This one will further help you to understand what each of the top 10 in your list mean to you.

Exercise:

- Take each value and ask the following questions

> ➤ What exactly does this mean to me?
> ➤ How would it look like tangibly?
> ➤ How would I know if I embody this value?

VII   *Congruence ratings:*

Exercise:

- Come up with a congruence rating for each value.
- On a scale of 1 to 10 how much are you living and embodying this particular value.
- You might discover that there is lot of gap in congruence.

VIII   *10/10*

Exercise:

- This is a very important visualisation exercise.
- What would it look for you to be at 10/10 congruence for all your values?
- Write them down in short paragraph format.

IX   *Prioritizing values:*

"You have to decide what your highest priorities are and have the courage – pleasantly, smilingly, non-apologetically to say 'no' to the other things. And the way you that is by having a bigger 'yes' burning inside." – Stephen Covey

Exercise:

- Take two values out of your list and ask the key question – Would 1 be more fulfilled with lots of value 1 but little value 2 or little value 1 but lots of value 2?
- Make this comparison with every value on the list.
- As you do this, you flip the most important ones at the top.
- Try to be more intuitive than logical – what does your gut tell you?

X   *Positive vs negative values:*

Positive vs negative motivation – some vales we are positively motivated towards and some values we are negatively motivated towards.

Exercise:

- Identify the negative motivations.
- Systematically remove the underlying causes of these negative motivations and replace with

positive ones OR at least let go of needing that value entirely.
- As example – Health for most people is negatively motivated due to extrinsic causes and it's not self-sustaining in the long run.
- Your negative motivations towards a value arises from deep rooted insecurities.
- Further, go on to find a positive / negative motivation ratio for each value.
- Mark the values that have over 50% negative motivation in them and try to identify one or two themes as to why these negative motivations are there.
- Common themes – avoiding loneliness, avoiding going broke, low self-esteem (deficient, unworthy, incapable, unlovable, not good enough), desperate need for love, intimacy, being liked and approved of.

XI *Conclusion:*

"A mission statement is not something that you write overnight…but fundamentally your mission statement becomes your constitution, the solid expression of your vision and values." – Stephen Covey

"It isn't normal to know what we want. It is a rare and difficult psychological achievement." – Abraham Maslow

This values list is the blueprint of your entire life and it tells you:

- What you really are.
- What you really want and why you want it.

Your life purpose is pretty much visible in your top 3 values. If these ten things are the most important to you then why would you be doing / pursuing anything else that does not align with this list? This is a fluid list but a very solid foundation. Put it in a safe place and maybe make multiple copies of it too.

XII *30 day challenge:*

- Review your list for 5 minutes each day.
- Chart yourself on a calendar and check off every single day you do.
- After 30 days are over, do at least one quarterly review.
- These values would just be castles in the air if they are not programmed into you.

CHAPTER TWENTY

THE VISION BOARD

"It's never wrong to tell yourself the truth about what you want, even though you may think it's not possible to have." – Robert Fritz

A vision is a long term big picture of how your life is going to unfold. To be more specific it is the cohesive, compelling, emotionally stirring and a bit idealistic picture of what the future holds for you.

Exercise:

- Dream for 20-30 minutes of all the various possibilities possible with your life purpose.
- Fill your notepad with all the cool stuff.
- Be idealistic and realistic at the same time.

Questions:

- Where could my life purpose take me if I went all out with it?
- How could I impact other people?
- What people specifically would I be impacting?
- How could I be a leader in my industry / business / career / field?

- Thinking about any fortunate breakthroughs / huge realisations that I could have on my journey?
- How will my personal life be affected by my career?
- How will it affect my relationships and hobbies?
- How will it affect my health, fitness and nutrition?
- How will it affect my financial situation?
- How will your identity change?

Tips:

- Don't let fear hold you back.
- The potential impact you will be having on society at large or that one person (or core inner circle) will really stick it for you.
- Focus on how good it would feel to live a life where you are sharing your greatest gifts with the world.
- Trust your intuition above all else.

"There is no passion to be found playing small – in settling for a life that is less than the one you are capable of living." – Nelson Mandela

Creating a vision board:

- The process of assimilation is perhaps the most important.
- Do this in a digital format.
- Open a really large canvas size.
- 1550 horizontal and 3200 height (recommended) – pixels
- Make sure you set 300 dpi (dots per minute)
- Pick 100s of images at first.
- Import to editing software.
- Each image on its own layer.
- Select the largest images possible from google (500 to 1000 pixels or more)
- *Scare yourself a little bit with your ambitions.*
- Post it in a place where you can see it a lot during the day.
- Most important of all – have fun with it!

CHAPTER TWENTY ONE

DEALING WITH FEAR

(when abiding to your vision in the course of your life)

"Your ego will set off a smoke bomb of fear. It will attempt to sabotage you by telling you tall tales of the terrors you will experience if you take the big leap into your zone of genius." – Gay Hendricks.

"Homeostasis is like gravity" – Unknown

- Fear is unavoidable. A coward will face petty fears and a hero would have fears in the face of a noble obstacle.
- Conquering fear – That's pretty much your whole mission.
- Fear is not the obstacle – It's the obstacle course.
- The first step – A lot of the power fear holds over us comes from not acknowledging it. Fears can be very deceptive and ridiculous.

Common fears:

- I will run out of money.

- I will fail again, just like I did last time.
- But it's going to be so discomforting to implement this change in my life.
- But it's going to need so much work.
- But my parents (family / friends) will hate me if I go down this route. What will they think of me? I know they are not going to accept it.
- I will be alone if I go towards my life purpose. I will get alienated from everyone around me.
- I might screw my life or family if I got down that route.
- I will embarrass myself. I will fall flat on my face and get laughed at.
- But I can't. I cannot have that difficult conversation that I need to with that person in my life, for what will they think of me?

Most monsters on the journey will be your own fears. Start to accept whatever fears you have as being created by you and not something external that's lurking like a monster in a bush. Looking back at a situation, it'll be almost laughable to you as to how you could have been so scared of that situation.

Remember:

- Facing a fear initially seems a lot scarier than it actually is.
- You know you have the capability to outgrow your fears, sometimes it just requires more knowledge / skill / support.

Action steps against fear:

Fear is one of the biggest obstacles in realising our vision. At its root, fear is an emotion that arises from negative thoughts about the future. When you anticipate future pain or suffering, you experience fear. Most of us have at least 2 to 3 major fears that control our lives. These fears almost always exist because at some point in our past, an event happened that caused us to feel lots of negative emotion and now we live actively to prevent that from reoccurring.

Exercise:

- What are the three things I fear most in my life?
- What is my #1 greatest fear in life?
- If my fear actually took place, what's the worst thing that could happen?
- If I actually happened, what would I ultimately have to do to deal with it?
- The fear was created to protect me from the reoccurrence of which negative event from the past?
- The thing I fear the most in my business or career?
- The things I habitually worry about the most are?

- How does my greatest fear hold me back from sharing my gifts with the world?
- What would my life look like if I let go of this fear?
- 5 possible real-world action steps that I could take to reduce the effect of this fear in my life?

CHAPTER TWENTY TWO

STOP BEING A VICTIM

(Empower yourself)

For this one, I would like you to select one area of your life where you are stuck and feel like a victim. Some victim / self-defeating thoughts go as, 'I can't', 'It's impossible', 'it just won't work in this situation', '<insert person/situation> is holding me back', 'I'm feeling so trapped'. So, where in your life do you feel like this? Could be with your marriage, relationship, children, career, business, health etc. Just select one, whether you are a total victim in life or just one specific area where you feel victimized. If you found it – good, now keep it mind as we'll be talking a bit here about victim mindsets.

So, what makes a victim, a victim? A victim thinks that the external world is a greater obstacle to him than he is to himself. It's critical that you grasp this because it's such a deep insight. What I'm telling you is that you are the only obstacle and there are no other obstacles, but you. Anything that you think is an external obstacle such as lack of money, lack of time, someone holding you back, the world being unfair or anything like these, is an illusion.

One of the bedrock foundational principles of self-development – your mind is the greatest obstacle. The problem of course is if you are a victim, you won't believe it. When I tell you this, your mind comes up with all sorts of objections, logic and counter examples which you believe are extremely convincing and refute what this foundational principle. That's not the case and I want to convince you of it as that understanding and introspection alone can help you to break out of the rut.

There are 3 levels at which you can grasp this:

- The surface level of just reading it and understanding it intellectually.
- The second level, little deeper where you actually get a little bit convinced of this principle.
- The third and really deep level of grasping this where you see how this is true for you and why it happens in you.

When I say that your mind is the greatest obstacle I'm not implying that the solution to everything is positive thinking. Victims don't really grasp this and cannot see the ramifications that such a statement has. In a victim, there's a failure to appreciate the possibility of self-deception and how much their own mind is deceiving them. If you're wise, you will take the possibility of self-deception very seriously.

Instead of worrying about the external world, what you should actually be worrying about is the following:

- Your mental filters, attitude, limiting beliefs and judgements.
- Unquestioned assumptions you have about reality.
- Lack of introspection.
- The content of the images that you run through your mind.
- You monkey mind and its non-stop internal dialogue.
- How your thoughts and beliefs are charged by emotional reactions and judgements.
- What you view as right / wrong and good / evil.
- Your self-constructed model of morality.
- The habits that you cultivate or lack thereof.
- Your self-talk. How do you talk to yourself? What words do you use and what's the tone of the language you use when you talk to yourself?
- Your mindfulness and ability to stay present.
- Your own ego and it's projections on the outer world.

These are things you should really be concerned about but as a victim you tend to discount them. You send most of your time worrying about the external world rather than the internal world. Another way I like to put it – you spend too much time worrying about physics rather than psychology. Reality or the external world as you call it is a projection of the internal world. You fail to acknowledge how much external reality is worked by your internal psychology.

What makes it difficult for you to extricate yourself from victimhood? If you are a victim to some facet of life or all of life then part of your internal world has a belief in it that says something along the following – how I think about the world is not that significant and I've got some real problems to deal with which you just don't understand. It's beautiful how deceptive your own mind is. When you think that your thoughts are not that significant you are actually giving this base thought maximum significance and relying on it to not introspect further into your thoughts and internal belief system. Due to this the victim fails to become aware of how majority of the obstacles are created by their own mind, attitude, beliefs and perspective.

Truth is that there is no problem which is absolute in the external world. A problem is a feature of the mind. Problems are projections of your mind because it you who attributes meanings to situations in the external world. You apply the parameters within your own mind and hold yourself as a hostage to reality. You give arbitrary external circumstances the remote control of your life.

Not just that, your mind keeps fuelling the problem continuously to keep it alive. A problem needs to be fed actively. Think of it like a creature that lives in your head and you constantly feed it to keep it alive. However, you are not consciously aware of the fact that you are feeding this problem. The deception and illusion of the problem have an external root cause is very strong and until you realise and witness this truth within yourself, you are going to be able to permanently let them go. Every avenue of solution that comes your way will be denied by your mind because your mind is searching for the answers in the wrong place.

Let us do a small thought experiment:

- Imagine for a moment that the inner world is all that matters in life. So, this would be pretty much the exact opposite of what you currently believe.
- Now if that were the case (it really is but since you don't conform to it consciously, allow yourself to consider it as a possibility) then changing things in the external wouldn't work, right?
- Fixing problems in the outer world would be equivalent to window dressing and any

problem that you do manage to fix would be temporary and reoccur in another form.

- This will create immense frustration giving you a feeling that the problem is insolvable.
- Now, what's funny is that didn't we just describe the exact situation in which you find yourself being a victim? Isn't that how your situation is right now?
- You keep changing the outer world (or at least you try to) but the problem keeps repeating over and over again with maybe slight variation.
- So, shouldn't this clue to towards the fact that it's the inner world that really matters.
- If you don't solve the problems in the inner world they will keep being projected outwards.

It's almost like as if you are at a movie at the theatre with the old-fashioned time projectors and then you notice a blip or smudge on the screen. You walk up to the screen and try to clean it up but it doesn't really go away. Why? Because the smudge is actually on the lens of the projector that gets projected on to the screen. So, you can clean the screen all you want but it wont help until you really go and clean the lens, back there. The 'I' has to start to look at itself so to speak.

Stop allowing your mind to frame control you. Frame control is kind of like your mind frames every situation, setting the foundations and parameters based on unquestioned assumptions.

Exercise: (pull out your notebook / do it in your head but vividly and spend sufficient time on each step)

- Select one area in your life where you feel the most victimized. Be specific about it and write it down.
- Note down all your justifications of why you cannot change in that area and also for why you think that it's not your fault.
- Now I want you to identify how the problem seems like an external problem.
- Then I want you to identify how the problem is actually an internal problem.
- Find that contrast. Find how your mind is being deceptive in this.
- Watch out for justifying that the problem is external rather than external.
- Ask the following question – how am I creating the obstacle? What am I avoiding by creating the obstacle?
- Final question – what must I believe to be a victim?

"The victim mindset dilutes the human potential. By not accepting personal responsibility for our circumstances, we greatly reduce the power to change them." – Steve Maraboli

"We all have been through a lot of sh*t in our lives; the difference is some of us choose not to play the victim." – Unknown

CHAPTER TWENTY THREE

DREAMKILLERS

(Busting negative beliefs)

This chapter is devoted to giving you extra traction that will help you to break out of your inertia and shatter the limiting beliefs that hold you back. The aim is here to get you to start living a really passionate life – the kind of life that you always dreamt off. Here, we will tackle the most important phase of it – gaining momentum and darting head on.

Our personal beliefs about reality and life determine where we can and where we can't go in life because they turn into self fulfilling prophecies. Maybe you want to earn a lot of money and move to a tropical island but another voice in your head keeps saying something along the lines of – ah that's fantasy, it's never going to happen, it's silly OR you're not good enough to make it happen and even if you did, you would end up screwing it up anyways. There are different subtle variations of how this your limiting beliefs could manifest and they come to us from bad past conditioning from our childhood and especially our adolescence. While these limiting beliefs might feel very real to you, they are actually false. What's worse is that they are disempowering, robbing you of energy and cutting off newer possibilities in life.

I've myself wrestled a quite a bit with my negative beliefs and still do once a while although majority of them have dissolved. Throughout this chapter we will delve into several negative and limiting beliefs that keep people stuck in rut. We will also walk through on how to reframe these believes so they start acting likes catalysts in your journey to greatness rather than hurdles. These reframes are not wishy washy, in the air optimistic ones. They are downright practical and very effective.

Your limiting beliefs might hold true in very narrow contexts but most people develop these blind spots thus colouring the same old and worn our brush. When you begin to reframe and apply them in real life, you will be awed as to how much you were being held back and deluding yourself previously. Your beliefs are like the map of a territory and while the territory is real, the map itself is just a schematic / model. Sometimes, the map is dangerously misleading as the territory keeps changing over time but the map keeps projecting it's outdated and skewed measurements upon it. What's really dangerous is how you convince yourself that all your negative and limiting beliefs are true.

I   Fear of failure:

This is a universal fear and all of us have it. I tend to assume (which is backed with facts) that no matter how developed you are personally, you are always going to have at least a tinge of fear of failure if not a lot of it. It's natural when you are pursuing something big, moving out of your comfort zone and the path being uncertain. Truth is that only if failure going to happen, it's going to happen a lot. You need to start reconditioning yourself and stop seeing failure as a bad thing.

Every time you fail, you learn a new lesson. Instead of viewing failure as a pushback, look at it as a feedback mechanism that is fuelling your success. You gaining valuable life experiences, you seeing what doesn't work to help you readjust and change or make course corrections. That's the only legit way you can ever become great at something – Trial and error. You won't achieve any perfection if you're diving head first with no expectations to fail or accepting failure with open arms.

It's shocking to see the number of times some of the most successful people in history have failed. Of course, we have got the classic Thomas Edison example of the 1,000 lightbulbs to support this. This is something more than a cliché. It's something that you have to really start to turn your mind on to.

Nowadays whenever I enter into something new, I expect to fail dozens. The only important thing is to keep pushing and reintegrating all the lessons into your current paradigm. Read of biographies of some of the most successful people and that will help you to reframe this stubborn belief. Don't forget that life does give you multiple attempts. We do have a tendency to put the job at hand on a pedestal and treat it like an ultimatum thus putting as at very tight and self-sabotaging spots. What's even more dangerous is the fear of failure preventing you from taking any action at all.

If you're looking at the very short-term picture then sure failure is a bad thing. But in long term (if you zoom out and take a look at a 5/10-year period) you will see that every attempt that you're failing is improving you and making you stronger and wiser. Remember that *it's very hard to fail in the long term* if you have strong vision and are living up to your values. That's why I encourage you to build a passionate life abiding in your core values as I know that it's the best way to minimise failure and the fear of failure.

"Fear kills more dreams than failure ever will." – *Unknown*

"There is only one thing that makes a dream impossible to achieve – Fear of failure." – *Paulo Coelho*

"Success is your ability to go from failure to failure without losing your enthusiasm." – Winston Churchill

II   Stuck in comfort:

Here's how this one tends to sound – But I've already got a decent life. Sure, I don't have my greatest dreams accomplished and the stuff that I dreamt in high school and college but I'm just comfortable right now. I've got an okay job, an okay relationship and so why don't I just continue with that? I don't really want to go out there and disturb this current bubble that I am in.

The problem with his mentality is that you are really selling yourself short. You are robbing yourself of all the possibilities and excitement in life. People who employ this strategy eventually realise that their highest self (which was responsible for all their big dreams and ambitions) is not going away. It's not going to just die. They maybe able to repress it and shove it in some dark corner but still that voice in the back of their mind will be whispering to them. This will make them miserable because over time it becomes like a splinter in the finger. Initially it may cause some irritation but if you let it fester, it starts to rot.

Abraham Maslow describes self-actualisation as a need and not as a luxury. You are never going to become fulfilled using this comfort seeking strategy – realise this. All the things about your life that you are tolerating right now are going to eat you up from within. Slowly as the years pass, you are going to get more jaded, falling flat on every dream and basically a victim of life. Not only will you feel guilty in the present moment knowing that you could be doing things of a much higher value but you will also have deep regrets on your deathbed for selling yourself short and seldom taking the leap. A life - half lived, so to speak. Don't be that guy who has a mid-life crisis at the age of 40 or 60. Start having them now, at your 20s / 30s and use them to propel your life exponentially.

"Life begins at the end of your comfort zone." – Neale Donald Walsch

"In any given moment we have two options: To step forward into growth or to step back into safety." – Abraham Maslow

"Are you truly happy or just comfortable?" – Unknown

III   The inauthentic self:

Here's how this one goes – But this isn't me. This is not who I really am. You're asking me to go out there and be this passionate and ambitious person… that's not who I am. It's not me to go out there and start something new or challenging.

You need to be careful about pigeon-holing yourself into negative labels or categories. As mentioned in a chapter above, trying to honour your own limiting mental labels is a cheap defensive tactic of the ego. An excuse to really stay stuck in life. To shut themselves off from new possibilities and experiences. You are not a static entity but instead the 'you' of who you are is dynamic and ever changing based on new experiences and inputs every moment. So, don't safeguard or harbour limiting beliefs or constraints about who you are and why cannot do certain things. The complacent attitude of "Well, that's who I am" is an excuse masquerading as arbitrary truth (groundless) to reason out your under achievements.

Consider that you don't really know who you are. People simply assume that they know everything about themselves they 'I am me'. No, actually you don't. Most people have no idea of who they are unless they go through some deep soul searching. How can you know who you are if you haven't even achieved a fraction of your maximum potential?

Don't be too eager to classify yourself or box yourself into mental labels to gain some sense of belonging or uniqueness. Recognise that the 'you' of who you are can change a lot and be ready for it. There is no fixed 'you' and never will be. Your memories don't stand as any evidence for a fixed 'you'. Changing some of these limiting beliefs can alter the core of your personality and you have to be ready to let a part of yourself die / burn in the process.

"Your authentic self is who you are when you have no fear, judgement or limiting constructs holding you back or before the world starts pushing you around and telling you who you are supposed to be." – Paul McGraw

IV   Setting a small goal:

This is so counter intuitive that most people get it wrong and here's how it goes – I'm going to set some 'realistic' goals. I like what you're talking about here regarding dreaming big but I'm not going to go all the way. I'm going to set these goals that 'I know I can accomplish'.

The danger is actually greater is setting a small goal than setting a big goal. When you set shallow goals that gradually modify into average visions, it's hard to get yourself motivated enough to actualize your true potential. Any goal requires a certain expenditure of effort, time, money etc to get it done. You might think that setting smaller goals will get them accomplished easily but that's the point. It is the fear of failure that is withholding you from taking a bigger leap. It's scaring you and therefore making you resist change and discomfort. A larger will mentally prepare you to leave your comfort zone and be open to experiencing failure thus making you more effective in pursuing your dreams. While this effectiveness might not be immediately noticeable (as compared to a small goal) but in the long run it will pay off exponentially.

You don't get inspiration from small, 100% sure shot achievable goals (although people think that small baby step achievements motivate you into moving forward but in the grand scheme of life it is a sheer waste of potential). That's not growth and in fact backslides you into complacency. You get inspiration from a big and deep compelling vision.

Don't worry about the 'how to' of your goal while setting it. This is something that a lot of people get tripped up on. 'How to' only works for a small goal because you are already sure of achieving it. Yes, it's important to chart out the potential check points but going into excessive details in the very beginning is detrimental to the vision itself. The brain wants to see all the intermediate steps the lead from A to Z and this is because of the fear of uncertainty. It wants to make sure that all the steps are more or less achievable and in sync with the current comfort zone. As you walk along the path more soaking up data, experience and lessons, you will be automatically equipped to take on challenges that await you in times of uncertainty.

If you can see the whole path clearly then your vision is pretty small. You need something to fill in those blanks in the grand vision? Take self trust. Trust in your abilities and potential. Trust in your future self. Because no matter what great task you take on, uncertainty is inevitable and sometimes the only thing that is certain.

"If you have a big vision, you can't afford to work with 'can't' and 'but' people." – Unknown

"Create the highest, grandest vision possible for your life because you become what you believe." – Oprah Winfrey

"Never give up on what you really want to do. The person with big dreams is more powerful than one with all the facts." – Albert Einstein

V   Fear that you are not good enough:

This is a very dangerous and limiting belief. Honestly, you don't really know if you are good enough or not and that's up to the journey to reveal. The obstacles in your journey will test your mettle and even if you get defeated by one of those obstacles then remember that it's just temporary. That pushback was needed to make forge you into a stronger version of yourself to fit the road ahead. You can always lick your wounds and come back even stronger.

The truth is that there is very little in life that you are inherently 'not good enough' to do. Your potential is literally infinite (as with any human being). A sobering thought – the average human being taps into less than 10% of their full potential. So, it's not like you are lacking in anything. In fact, if it's anything then it's the drive and motivation which you need to build in yourself. No matter what you think you're lacking in (and how much), you can always develop it or use the other variables to cover up for it. That's the whole point of growing as a human being.

The inner resources that you have as a human being to mobilize yourself, to build deep passion, to engage your focus and energy and a strong vision is more important than any external resource. It's always within you and accessible at will. If you want something bad enough then you will develop yourself good enough. If you have a 5-year term goal and are clueless about how to proceed now then don't assume that the remaining 5 years will be spent in moving at this same current pace. Once you have gained momentum and traction and built a solid foundation then the wheel will roll much faster.

"Limitless is your potential. Magnificent is your future." – Gordon B Hinckley

"I am always doing things I can't do. That's how I get to do them." – Pablo Picasso

"There is no man living who isn't capable of doing more than he thinks he can do." – Henry Ford

"You are confined only by the walls you build yourself." – Unknown

VI Lack of time:

"I don't have time to pursue my dreams because <excuse> keeps me so busy." The reason you don't get enough time is because you are failing to properly prioritize your schedule. This makes you run around like a hamster on a wheel spending majority time doing things which you have low emotional attachment towards, more often than not fulfilling someone else's agenda. So, yes you are busy but busy with the wrong stuff thus sacrificing on your own values.

The 80/20 rule that is proven to work even in concrete physical systems implied that 80% of the really good output (results) in any system tend to come from only 20% of the input. That means 20% of what you're doing is generating 80% of your results. Therefore, the remaining 80% is excess that can be trimmed off as it's producing a mere 20% of results. You can cut a lot of unnecessary things out of your life and you will not hamper your productivity. This will free up your schedule but still keep you productive. This allows you to take the 20% activities and expand them and invest more time in them.

Most of the 'busy' people are like short sighted war generals who are so desperate to win the battle at hand that they lose sight of how everything plays out in the large war. Basically, busy with immediate details that don't serve the larger vision much. We fail to see how this particular battle is not really important in the big picture and can be abandoned.

"Those who ignore the 80/20 principle are doomed to average returns. Those who use it must bear the burden of exceptional achievement." – Richard Koch

"Resist the urge to clear up small things first." – Brian Tracy

VII   Too old to change:

This is such a crippling belief and I'm sure that we all have it at some point. Whenever we find a great thing, we always wish that we had started earlier. You can go out there and find amazing people who have succeeded in the twilight of their lives. Since you are always learning and growing, age is just an arbitrary measurement that shouldn't be looked up as an absolute. Remember that you're only in a race with yourself and not with others.

Modern day neuroscience has shown that the brain has a lot of plasticity and that you can strengthen neurons and alter its plasticity even after long periods of time. If you are passionate about it and want it bad enough then it's never too late.

"And it's never too late to start something new, to do the things you've been longing to do." – Dallas Clayton

"It's never too late to start over. If you weren't happy with yesterday then try something different today. Don't stay stuck. Do better." – Andy Wooten

"It's never too late to turn things around. You are the only obstacle." – Dave Ramsey

VIII   Too invested:

Here's how this one goes – Are you telling me that I am going down a dead end? Yes, I have dreams but I have been investing so much time and energy into this current career (which you settled for). I can't just throw it all away and start from scratch.

Its true that we can spend years of our life investing lots of time, energy and our soul into something that does not align with our highest aspirations and only later realising the same. This is scary because it's hard to admit this to yourself especially when you have been so invested in it. The more time you invest, the more it feels like – Ah, I don't want to admit it. The truth is that you are not restarting from scratch when you change tracks. It's important to move around and tinker in the world we live to explore more potential possibilities and realise our dreams. You cannot just be born, go to school, go to college and know exactly what to do without going down any dead ends.

In reality most people fumble around, make mistakes, get into bad relationships, fail at businesses, plunge into different careers and all this gives them immense wisdom and insight about themselves, situations and life in general. If you realise that the direction is not right for you then you should switch. If you know that this thing right now is not right for you are you going to just tolerate it? Well there is that impulse – ah, you know what it's good enough. Will you really spend the rest of your existence in this mediocre and half aligned career / whatever the situation is? Do you really want to be going down a dead end knowing that it's a dead end already? Basically, doubling down on your wrong bet. Even though in the short term it is painful to admit your folly and make the course correction, in the long run you will be more than glad that you had the courage to do that.

"Making a big life change is scary. But you know what's scarier? Regret." – Unknown

"Real vision demands that we make tough choices. Real vision is responsible and is paid for." – Michael F Easley

IX   It's up to fate:

Here's how this goes – But if I was really meant to be successful then it would happen naturally. Why should I have to push myself so hard?

If you study the lives of great achievers throughout history then you will discover that they never left anything up to fate. They didn't leave their life in the hands of a random chance. They were very proactive about how they pursued their dreams / results. If you have a dream that's very dear to you then what are the chances that it will manifest naturally? What are the chances of it falling right into your lap? Instead of playing a passive role in life, let's play an active role - the one of a creator. The natural / default is mediocre. Self actualisation and reaching your highest potential is not easy and therefore demands you to forgo your natural state.

"Luck's just another word for destiny. Either you make your own or you're screwed." – John Le Carre

"You can stand around and wait to be asked to dance." – Amy Poehler

"Don't wait for the stars to align. Reach up and arrange them the way you want." – Pharrell Williams

X   Maybe later:

Here's how this one goes – I love all these ideas that you are throwing at me. I have these goals and a grand vision for myself but I'll start it later.

If you are not ready to do something now (when the excitement and eagerness is fresh) then let's face it... when are you going to? If you put it off for 6 or 12 months is it going to make it more likely or less likely that you will follow through with it? It's true that sometimes the external circumstances force us to postpone but what I find is the most of the people turn a necessary postpone into a long procrastination with heaps of reasons and excuses that prevent them from taking action.

There is always resistance to doing something great with our life because that means we have to go out there and push our comfort zone. Overcoming that would be getting one of the biggest obstacles out of your way. So, why do you want to delay your passion and dreams?

"You cannot escape the responsibility of tomorrow by evading it today." – Abraham Lincoln

ABOUT THE AUTHOR

"Stop acting so small, you are the whole universe vibrating in an ecstatic motion." – Rumi

My passion for writing and philosophising has taken me to myriad lanes in life. Couple that with an obsessive search for truth, meaning and purpose that is never satiated enough. Well, I'm just a regular guy who happened to step into the journey of self-discovery and true knowing. I learnt and discovered so much, everyday was a learning curve, every moment a tutor.

I love helping people uncover the truth and look deeper into themselves. Nothing can brighten my day more than helping a person realise their true authentic self beneath all the fluff and egoic exterior. To have them stand in awe and walk out with intense passion and zeal for existence.

I'm 23 years of age, an ENTP and currently pursuing my further education from Mumbai, India. My hobbies include debating, reading, cooking, music, investing, spirituality and helping people rise out of their ruts.

I'm so glad to have finally written my first book – A dream come true for me. But this is just the beginning…

I truly hope that this book has left a mark on you and infused you with a higher degree of self-awareness. If you have any queries or suggestions, feel free to contact me. *Further if you need private counselling (completely free of cost) I'll be more than willing to help you.*

Contact:

pranoyentp@gmail.com

10576299R00111

Printed in Great Britain
by Amazon